Marked Cards

BY THE SAME AUTHOR

By Victories Undone

EMMANUEL OLYMPITIS

Marked Cards

A RAUCOUS MEMOIR OF GLITTERING TIMES IN INTERNATIONAL BUSINESS

For Wilfred

Merry Christmas!

with best wishes

Manoli.

QUARTET BOOKS

First published in 2020 by Quartet Books Limited
A member of the Namara Group
27 Goodge Street, London, W1T 2LD

A catalogue record for this book is available from the British Library

ISBN 9780704374782

Typeset by Tetragon, London
Printed and bound in Great Britain by TJ International Ltd, Padstow, Cornwall

For Emily, and all the children.

'Open your mouth and shut your eyes
and see what Zeus will send you.'

ARISTOPHANES, *The Acharnians*

Contents

Prologue

IT WAS LATE SPRING 1985 IN MAYFAIR. I HAD EXCHANGED A dull-but-worthy, black-tie charity dinner in the Dorchester Hotel for the bar at Annabel's and was surrounded by my former dining companions. Like the dinner, they were worthy, but dull.

Bored witless, not tired, I slowly downed a large scotch with ice. Perhaps there was an amusing friend in the restaurant. I wandered through the swing doors, leaving the braying voices behind me. Standing still for a few moments, I glanced around the lamp-lit tables.

With a start, I saw, facing outwards at a corner table, the unmistakable features of Kirk Douglas. I knew Kirk quite well and liked him a great deal. He was an engaging, articulate person. He, with his wife, Ann, were close friends of my former mother-in-law – they stayed with her when they visited New York. I had dined with them on several occasions. The woman sitting opposite Kirk had her back to the room, so I couldn't see her. There was another man next to her, also with his back to the room. Beside Kirk was a strikingly beautiful woman with a blonde mane whom I didn't immediately recognise, but who looked familiar.

I approached Kirk, my hand extended.

'Manoli! Great to see you,' he exclaimed, looking up. 'How are you? Sit down, have a drink with us.' I accepted gratefully.

'Do you know Farrah Fawcett? Greg and Veronique Peck?' Kirk waved expansively at his guests.

It so happened that I did know Farrah quite well – she with her boy-friend Ryan O'Neal had been occasional guests of my ex-wife's – and I had once been seated next to Veronique Peck at a lunch in the South of France. But I had never met Gregory Peck. He was not only one of my favourite actors, but one of my heroes since childhood; like so many others, I had sat entranced through *The Guns of Navarone* and *To Kill a Mockingbird* several times. And he was as courteous and charming as his on-screen persona. As I drank another scotch, my mood soared. I was enjoying the lively, warm conversation as well as the impressed faces of the waiters, all of whom knew me well.

Not to overstay my welcome, fifteen minutes later I thanked Kirk for his hospitality and left them to finish their dinner in peace. I returned to my seat in the bar rather more inebriated than when I left.

'Where were you?' a couple of companions asked.

'Oh, just having a drink with some friends in the restaurant.'

'Anyone we know?'

'I shouldn't think so,' I replied smugly.

The noise, the inconsequential conversation, the smoke of scores of cigars and cigarettes was becoming oppressive. It was time to go home. At that moment, the swing doors from the restaurant opened to reveal Kirk Douglas and Farrah Fawcett departing. A sudden quiet descended as they made their way through the bar.

'Manoli!' Kirk called, 'See you soon in New York, I hope.' He held his arms out, and I went over for a Hollywood hug. I exchanged the oblig-atory kisses on the cheek with Farrah before they left.

People started to shout at me, 'Kirk Douglas! Wow, Farrah Fawcett!' and so on for a few minutes, which I brushed off with an insouciance I knew would irritate them. Gradually, the excitement passed, more cham-pagne was consumed, and the normal order of Annabel's bar at one in the morning was restored.

Now I would wait. Approximately twenty minutes later, the impres-sive frame of Gregory Peck appeared in the doorway of the restau-rant before he ambled amiably through the bar. You could hear the metaphoric pin drop. I sat as still as a stone. Hoping. Chuckling silently in anticipation.

'Goodnight, Manoli,' he waved as he strolled past me.

Yes. YES! I shouted inwardly, trying not to whoop aloud. What a Gent! 'Goodnight, Greg. See you soon,' I waved back with studied casualness and a ludicrously affected familiarity while he continued on his way.

All hell broke loose. Everyone shouted at me. Then everyone, it seemed, started to throw napkins and crisps and peanuts and cigarettes at me.

Tears of laughter streamed down my cheeks. I arose, bowed to one and all, waved regally, and departed, weaving slightly. I laughed myself to sleep that night. I have never enjoyed a charity dinner as much again.

CHAPTER ONE

Before I Forget ...

D EAR READER, I AM BY NO MEANS FAMOUS. YOU WILL HAVE
heard of me only if you were a follower of the gossip columns
or the financial press in London and New York from the early 1970s to
the early 2000s.

However, I have regaled my friends with so many anecdotes of my
life that they have persuaded me to write them down before I forget
them. Whether they hope this will stop me endlessly telling them, I
am not sure.

These stories are of their time. I have been extremely lucky in coming
across such people. The cast of characters will certainly be familiar; it
is drawn from the business world, show business, music, writing, and
what is loosely termed society – or, perhaps more accurately, café society.

The 1960s, '70s, '80s, and '90s have now passed into folk lore. The
excitement of so many innovations in music, the arts, travel, education,
and fashion shaped exhilarating times for those with the good fortune
to enjoy them. As a gambler, I have been increasingly convinced that
throughout my life I have been playing with a hand of marked cards.
Cards marked by a benevolent Fate. For, through a combination of luck
and timing, I had not only a ringside seat but also the privilege of meeting
many of the legendary characters that forged those times. I was blessed
to have been at university in the late 1960s and in my twenties, thirties,
and forties in the successive decades.

I hope you will read on. I do not regard this short work an autobiography, although every word is true. Please treat it as a light-hearted memoir, written more in the form of a novel or a collection of short stories. Generally I have tried to keep events in chronological order, but as often happens when talking about one's own life, one thing leads to another, suddenly I'm twenty years ahead of myself, and the sequencing goes temporarily awry. Please indulge me in these deviations, they are quickly corrected.

I have no intention of imposing upon you the standard several chapters of my early life. Norman Mailer, my close friend and mentor, once told me that a reader becomes bored three pages before he or she realises it, and that once this has dawned, the book that is put down is rarely picked up again. If you have read this far, I dare not stop you. So here goes, to set the scene as it were, in not more than three pages.

I was born in London in December 1948 and brought up in Dulwich Village – then a picturesque village just outside South London, on the borders of Kent. My parents came from the island of Kalymnos, which in the year of my birth had finally been reunited with Greece after thirty-five years as an Italian colony and, for some 500 years prior to that, a subject of the Ottoman Empire. Mountainous Kalymnos is one of the larger Dodecanese Islands. Close to the Turkish coast, it was for several centuries the centre of the world's natural-sponge industry. At that time the great majority of its population of 12,000 was employed within it. They enjoyed a level of prosperity which was unparalleled in the Eastern Aegean.

My great, great-grandfather Emmanuel Olympitis (after whom I was named) was the largest landowner on the island, the leading natural sponge merchant, and was elected its first mayor in the mid-1800s. He developed the central residential neighbourhood of the capital town, built the main cathedral, was responsible for the consolidation of the disparate parts of the sponge industry, and became a prime negotiator in a treaty with the Sultanate of Turkey, under which all the Dodecanese Islands received favourable tax status. Emmanuel Olympitis was given the honorific title of Archon ('ruler') by the Turkish government, while the duty-free status of the Dodecanese Islands continued right through their reunification with Greece. This only ended with the country's accession to the European Union in 1981.

My great-grandfather, John Olympitis – together with his brother-in-law Nikos Vouvalis – sent sponge divers to live as far afield as Tarpon Springs in Florida, Nassau in the Bahamas, and Cuba, thereby extending the annual harvest beyond the Mediterranean. The descendants of these communities still live and flourish in the Bahamas and Florida. John and Nikos were active in their patronage of Kalymnian politics and their philanthropic support of local needs.

Three schools, an orphanage, an old people's home, and a large hospital were built in Kalymnos by one or other of the brothers-in-law, and in the late 1920s, the London office of J. E. Olympitis & Son was established to support the high volume of retail and commercial sponge trade with the United Kingdom. The more dynamic Vouvalis had founded his own N. Vouvalis & Co. in London at the turn of the twentieth century, and such had been its success that he was made a Freeman of the City of London. Family legend relates that he dined at Buckingham Palace as a guest of Queen Victoria, but I have no idea whether this is true.

My great-grandfather John died in his late nineties when I was seven years old. I remember him dimly now, but I do recall well a piece of advice he once gave me: 'Manolaki, never go into politics yourself. You make yourself a target. Much better to own the mayor than to be the mayor.' I have always been fascinated by politics, but never tempted to try.

Speaking of Greek politics, I'm reminded of a story my dear friend Nicholas Soames – with whom we have holidayed in Greece several times – once told me about his grandfather, Winston Churchill.

During the winter of 1944, as the Germans were withdrawing from Greece, the Foreign Secretary Anthony Eden approached Churchill.

'Winston, we must travel to Athens as a matter of the utmost urgency. The Greek Cabinet is about to convene for the first time to choose an interim prime minister pending elections. It is vital that we put our influence behind the candidate most friendly to Britain. The interim premier will have great influence over the elections, we must ensure Greece remains within our sphere of influence. A civil war with the Communists is coming.'

Churchill agreed. A Liberator bomber was readied to accommodate passengers. The next morning they clambered into the fuselage, Churchill wearing a heavy fur coat against the cold – a gift from Stalin – with an enormous cigar in his mouth despite the highly inflammable aviation fuel. Eden proposed they should swing their weight behind Archbishop Damaskinos. He had been the spiritual leader of the Greek people throughout the brutal German occupation, had spoken out bravely against the many atrocities, and resisted as much as possible the deportation of the Greek Jewish community to the concentration camps.

'Tell me, Anthony,' asked Churchill, 'about this Damaskinos. This Archbishop. Is he a God-fearing Christian of the finest sort, an honest, straightforward, righteous man of the cloth? Or is he a scheming, deceitful, and untrustworthy cleric?'

'I rather fear, Winston, he is the latter.' Eden shifted nervously.

'Excellent,' roared Churchill, 'he's our man!' And the rest, as they say, is history.

Anyway, I digress. My father, also John Olympitis, matriculated from the Italian boarding school in Rhodes, and then studied in Rome, Brussels, and London. He served with distinction in the Second World War as a junior officer of the Greek Brigade attached to the Long Range Desert Group, in action alongside British comrades in North Africa, the Aegean, and Italy. He was demobbed in Palestine, decorated with the Hellenic Cross for Valour, and came to London in 1946 to run the office.

In the meantime, he had met my mother, Argyro Theodorou. She had been born in London, but her family also came from Kalymnos. They had established themselves as sponge merchants first in Vienna, then in London. My mother attended Malvern Girls' College in Worcestershire and then the Royal Academy of Music. I will never forget how her stunning soprano voice and her wonderful piano playing lit up my childhood.

And so, it seemed quite natural that after nine years at Dulwich College Preparatory School, I should be sent off to board at The King's School, Canterbury. My time at both schools was extremely happy, if not particularly distinguished, except perhaps in one small aspect: I was a pretty good all-rounder in both academics and sports (not, alas, in music), but I was particularly good at fencing.

I led King's to victory for the first time in the 1966 Public Schools Fencing Championship, coming second in the individual Épée Championship and a finalist in the Foil. This competition (the Pearson Cup) had been dominated by Harrow and Eton for generations, but neither have won it since. In that same year, I became the only schoolboy before or since to win both the Kent Men's Open (Amateur and Professional) Foil and Épée championships simultaneously, after which I was a regular member of the Kent County Men's Team. In 1967, I came fourth in the National Junior Épée Championships, and thus entered the GB squad for the World Youth Championships. This – together with frequent appearances in the final stages of the annual major men's national competitions – resulted in my later sporadic inclusion in various GB national and Olympic squads during my undergraduate years. King's is now a 'centre of excellence' for schoolboy fencing, arguably the best in the country, and attracts students from all over the world. I am proud to have been one of the initiators of this.

Fencing, a somewhat arcane sport, often is described as playing chess at lightning speed. It requires the ability to think many moves ahead, together with speed, fitness, and exceptional reflexes. I have often wondered whether any of these attributes have affected my life. Perhaps they had a hand in the fact that, at least to date, I have been extremely fortunate in enjoying excellent health and fitness and have survived the politics of the world of finance, but then again, maybe not.

My younger brother, Nikitas, followed in my footsteps by becoming captain of fencing at King's. He gave up after university, but took it up again many years later, ultimately winning a team silver medal in the Commonwealth Games at the age of nearly forty. He was subsequently a non-fencing captain of the England team for some years.

My relationship with both Niki and my parents was extremely close. Tragically, my mother died of cancer at a young age, when I had just finished university. I have missed her enormously ever since. My father, an erudite and articulate linguist, was a handsome, stylish man, full of charm. He taught me a lot about politics and the Classics in particular. An excellent poker player, he also taught me the finer points of that game, and they have stood me in good stead all my life. John Olympitis was a pillar of the Greek community in London. He served as a church-warden of the Greek Orthodox Cathedral of the Divine Wisdom (Hagia Sophia) in Moscow Road, Bayswater, then as a founding trustee of St. Andrew's Greek Orthodox Cathedral in Kentish Town for forty years. He was appointed an Archon of the Patriarchate of Constantinople by the Patriarch in 1990. My father's life was full, long, and vital right up to the end. A fabulous grandfather, he died at ninety-four years of age, five years ago. I can hardly believe he has gone.

Norman Mailer's dreaded three pages before boredom loom large. Bear with me please, I'm almost there.

In 1967 I went up to University College London to read Law and began three fantastic years of enjoying London in the 'Swinging Sixties' and discovering girls who were themselves discovering the sexual liberation of the time. Miniskirts and hot pants abounded. Attitudes matched. I had many girlfriends, made many good friends of both sexes, and by the end of my studies had become a member of Annabel's and Tramp, where I spent many evenings, courtesy of a decent (but not too generous) allowance from my father. My academic work, I'm afraid, came a distant third behind girls and gambling. Unsurprisingly, its third place as a priority became a number which was to equal the class of my Law degree …

I had begun to play poker regularly. Initially in games with pals in the Students Union, then graduating to the smaller London casinos. The stakes were always a little higher than I could afford, but where was the excitement otherwise? This adrenalin was my mantra. Gambling in general began to gather a certain momentum that would last most of my life, the stakes increasing exponentially with my income as the years passed.

I'm sure you've heard enough about my early years, so I'd like to recount two asides on the subject of gambling. As Lord Byron observed in Canto XIV of *Don Juan*, 'In play, there are two pleasures for your choosing / The one is winning, and the other losing', and indeed I have won quite a lot of money through gambling and gained lifelong friendships, but equally I have felt the despair of losing, as these two stores illustrate.

Of course, for those with an addictive personality, gambling can easily become compulsive. Then it is a disease.* For myself, whilst I have an excessive streak of self-indulgence, I am normally strictly self-controlled when I need to be. I have almost always managed to contain my own stakes to keep any losses well within affordability. After all, for most Greeks gambling runs in the blood. But one night in the mid-1980s I had a narrow escape.

Frustrated by an early, devastatingly bad run at the blackjack table at Aspinalls, I made the fatal mistake of too rapidly increasing my stakes in an effort to recoup, instead of being patient and leaving whenever I reached an acceptable limit of losses. Like a punch-drunk boxer, I kept climbing back off the floor to absorb more punishment. I lost control.

---

* For centuries in Kalymnos, the vessels carrying the divers who harvest the natural sponges from the bottom of the ocean have gone to sea for six months at a time. The captains risked their own lives and endured great hardships, and it was not uncommon for several divers and crew to lose their lives during these largely successful quests for a good harvest. Such cargos have brought families involved in the industry considerable prosperity. But many families of these brave, macho men have been left literally destitute by the high-stakes gambling that traditionally takes place on the island between Christmas and New Year.

In a fevered state, I cashed cheque after cheque (unfortunately my credit was good), leaving at around two in the morning virtually hypnotised by my losses. I walked into my small flat at Eaton Place in total disbelief at what I had done. I was writing a novel at the time* and living on capital from the sale of my US business interests; I had no income, and yet I had lost an amount that is significant by even today's standards thirty years later. I could just about pay it, but it was a serious financial blow. And for what? How? Why? It was insane.

Bewilderment gave way to fury, which gave way to sober assessment. I was sick, I concluded. I must be. I must need help. I picked up the phone, called directory enquiries, and dialled the number for Gamblers Anonymous with calm deliberation. I badly needed to talk to someone. Instead I got a recorded message asking me to leave my number and informing me of the office hours: nine to five. My fury returned with a vengeance. Cursing, I hurled my telephone against a wall, smashing it. I kicked a small chair across the room, splintering one of its legs. Then I sat quietly, thinking, my head in my hands. There was only one thing for it. It was two-thirty in the morning and the casino closed at four, I wouldn't be able to sleep, I would return, cash one more cheque. In for a penny ...

This was the absolute worst decision I could make. But I got incredibly lucky. I did return, cashed my last cheque, sat at the punto banco table this time, and hardly lost a hand for half an hour. With reckless abandon I kept doubling my bets, and I kept winning. I soon recouped all my drastic losses. I moved to the roulette table. My streak continued. Suddenly I was thousands of pounds ahead on the evening. I had done it. Out of trouble completely, with money to spare. In a different kind of trance this time, I put 200 pounds on number 19, my lucky number, stood up, and called for my chips to be taken away and counted. As I was organising this, 19 came up, winning me 7,000 thousand pounds. Almost absent-mindedly I doubled the bet to 400 pounds, and moved towards

* Manoli Olympitis and Raymond Lewis, *By Victories Undone*, London: Quartet Books, 1988.

the cash desk. I had hardly gone ten yards when 19 repeated. A few other gamblers applauded: All losers at that time in the morning, it gave them hope. Another 14,000 pounds was added to my winnings. I had my back to the tables, discussing the cheque I was about to receive with the cashier, when the room exploded as number 19 came up for the third time in a row. I smiled ruefully, because I didn't have a bet on it this time. But of course I did! I had forgotten to take off the 400 pounds won before. The last three bets alone on number 19 had won another 35,000 pounds. I was mesmerised. The entire evening had become a weird dream. I went home and passed out. All I could think as I lost consciousness was to hell with Gamblers Anonymous: Thank God they were closed. But in the cold light of day, the next morning, I realised how extremely fortunate I had been. What a bullet I had dodged. I still get chills remembering that night. It taught me a lesson I will never forget, that this could happen to anyone.

Poker also led me to befriend some well-known public faces throughout my life. One such friendship was struck up as recently as 2002 as a result of playing in a weekly game.

In my St James's Club a private poker game began in the mid-1980s. It took place on Monday evenings, lasting for some twenty years. In its heyday, this game was considered to contain the highest stakes in London, and as you would expect, the players were an eclectic group of businessmen, theatrical impresarios, landowners, and investment bankers. One such player, who rarely lost, was an engaging entrepreneur – the aristocratic founder of a highly successful designer wallpaper business called Osborne & Little. His name was Sir Peter Osborne, and he was a good friend. During a break in the game one evening, Peter approached me with a request. His son George had recently been elected to Parliament to represent the constituency of Tatton in Derbyshire. Peter understood that my wife, Emily, and I were renting a cottage in the Peak District from Lord Derby, so would we be kind enough to ask George over for lunch one day? He knew few people in the area outside the Conservative Association, had a young family as we did, and would like to branch out a little. I was happy to help.

A few weeks later, an extremely youthful Member of Parliament arrived with his wife Frances at our 'Bothy', as the cottage was known. We had invited Teddy and Cazzy Derby to lunch as well to meet them. Everyone got on extremely well. This was to be the first of many such jolly times. Over the following years, George and Frances would become so close to the four of us that they would sell their house in Derbyshire, share the Bothy with us, and ultimately take it over from us when we left London for Wiltshire. We all spent many happy weekends together during which all our children became close. We included everyone's parents and in-laws whenever they stayed.

And so it happened that when George became Chancellor of the Exchequer, we were sharing the Bothy at weekends. Although Dorneywood House, Buckinghamshire – the Chancellor's official country residence – now became available to them, for quite a long time George, Frances, and the children preferred the informality of Derbyshire. It was also convenient for George to attend his constituency surgery from there on Fridays. We all carefully refrained from commenting on or asking George about political issues over the weekends out of respect for the short amount of leisure time available to him, unless he initiated such a conversation, which was rare. So, I cannot give you any insights, except that I believe I may have been helpful in formulating some of the ideas behind the new pension freedoms introduced by the Chancellor in an early budget. It was a hobbyhorse I could never resist flogging to anyone.

In London on the other hand, George and the family moved relatively quickly into the seat of power – the spacious flat above 10 Downing Street; David Cameron and his family had taken the larger flat above number 11. But it was before this move that George invited the Derbys and us for a takeaway dinner in a meeting room downstairs, which ended with a fascinating visit to the Cabinet Room in Number 10. I had not realised that the doors to numbers 10 and 11 Downing Street were effectively two entrances to the same large, double house. I learned with interest from a reliable source that apparently, during the Blair years, Gordon Brown had made sure that the door connecting the hallway which ran down the front of the two houses was kept locked, whereas the close relationship between George and David Cameron ensured it was kept open permanently.

After they moved in, George and Frances were kind enough to ask us to dinner at the flat on several occasions. George took enormous patriotic pride in showing guests his favourite historical objects in both houses. It was fascinating to me to try, unsuccessfully, to sit at William Pitt's tiny writing desk, which proved how small he really was, and walk down that famous staircase with its portraits of all the prime ministers, and to recline in Churchill's favourite armchair. William Pitt, I believe, is George Osborne's hero as well as mine. Both Pitt the Younger and Churchill were great wartime leaders, but Pitt – the youngest man to become Prime Minister at only twenty-four in 1759 – was a remarkable peacetime leader as well. He held that office for some twenty years, throughout which he was simultaneously Chancellor of the Exchequer, establishing Britain as the great maritime power that defeated Napoléon Bonaparte at the Battle of Trafalgar in 1805. Without his careful husbandry of the nation's finances for decades before, this would have been impossible. I am sure that explains George's admiration for him.

It was fortunate that Emily had known David Cameron well from childhood. Their fathers were close friends, her brother, Toppo Todhunter, had been Dave's best man and vice versa, and he was godfather to Ivan, Dave and Samantha's son who died at a tragically early age. So George was relaxed about us bumping into the PM in a corridor after dinner.

On the occasion of George's fortieth birthday party in 2011, we were invited to Dorneywood and subsequently stayed the night. Virtually the entire Cabinet was present, together with several political journalists and many old friends of George. William Hague made a typically witty speech in which he referred to 'Osborne's First Law of Politics'. This, he explained, was the uncanny ability to spot the next leader of the Conservative Party, attach himself closely to him, and make himself indispensable. Of course, prior to working with Cameron, George had been an assistant to Hague and also to Michael Howard.

This was the beginning of the age of austerity, during which Emily – a talented interior decorator – was summoned to serve her country. George commissioned her to redecorate some of the official rooms of 11 Downing Street for no fee at all, and, typically of her, she happily complied.

George's forty-fifth birthday party was a little different. It took place in Number 10, with many of the same guests, including some opposition MPs who were friends; I seem to recall Ed Balls as one. But, although a good party, it was not as relaxed as Dorneywood had been. In fact, there was a slight tension in the air. I soon realised that the host, David Cameron, was leaving in the morning to visit Angela Merkel. It was 2016. This was to be the ill-starred negotiation prior to the referendum. I wished the Prime Minister luck as I left, but despite his easy-going manner, I thought I could detect a trace of understandable anxiety. None of us there that night could have had any inkling of the titanic events and struggles that lay ahead. However, this is a major digression, I'm way ahead of myself.

CHAPTER TWO

The Transformative Sixties

I AM OFTEN ASKED ABOUT THE 1960S. WHAT WAS LIFE REALLY LIKE then? Was it all it has been cracked up to be? The answer to the last question, at least as seen through the eyes of an eighteen-to-twenty-one-year-old, is a resounding *YES*. But who does not look back at those formative years of one's life through rose-tinted spectacles? However, I feel I should add a short personal view of this decade that transformed all our lives.

For me, the Sixties began when England won the FIFA World Cup in 1966. This was a fabulous moment in itself after which anything seemed possible. The televised match which I watched was in black and white, but my memories of it are in the glorious Technicolor into which it was transformed a couple of years later. From that time, whenever I think back, I think in bright colours. The blaze of colours worn by the boys and girls that thronged the King's Road and Carnaby Street: preening peacocks, posing before psychedelic, rainbow shopfronts and unisex boutiques. Small, brightly painted sports cars raced around everywhere. That was the Sixties to me.

London was a kaleidoscopic hive of high-octane energy, and unisex was the style. Girls tended to dress boyishly, men quite effeminately. If a girl was wearing trousers, it could often be difficult to distinguish the sexes from close behind. Both young men and women wore flared, later full bell-bottomed trousers, closely fitted shirts, short scarves knotted around their necks, with wide leather belts outside their sweaters to accentuate narrow hips.

I remember that my favourite pair of suede trousers was severely flared from the knee and tight around the thighs. For shoes, I wore one of several pairs of high-heeled Chelsea boots, bought from the Chelsea Cobbler on the King's Road. I invariably wore a belt around my hips not waist.

Women tended to either grow their hair long over their shoulders and down their backs, or close cropped in an elfin style which was particularly suited to miniskirts or hot pants. These two hair styles were echoed by men. They either had really long hair over the shoulders as well, or a shorter, shaggy cut that covered the ears and dovetailed into a kind of mullet around the neck. This was my style, and I genuinely didn't see my ears properly (except when washing my hair) until I started to appear in court in the early 1970s. Indeed, washing hair for most men became at least a once-a-day necessity to keep hair both manageable and clean.

Speaking of hair, I can vividly recall celebrating the morning of my nineteenth birthday by treating myself to a haircut before lunch at the ultra-fashionable (and expensive) Sweeney's in Beauchamp Place. A very different place to the traditional high-street barber's shop, I nervously entered a dimly lit basement, reverberating with 'Nights in White Satin' by the Moody Blues, bustling with striking mini-skirted girls. Instantly, I was surrounded by three of the pretty assistants together with the celebrity hairdresser – a new form of celebrity. My hair was showered, shampooed, rinsed, my order for coffee and a toasted sandwich taken. Sitting back comfortably, I had recovered my nerve and was beginning to feel very much at home, when sudden, jubilant shouts of 'Terry! Terry! Hi, Terry mate!' followed my abrupt abandonment for some considerable time. My dripping wet hair became uncomfortably cold that December morning. My coffee and my sandwich never did appear. Terence Stamp had just walked in.

There was everywhere a feeling of great optimism, the firm belief that life was one terrific party, throughout which none of us would ever become old. That life must be embraced with complete freedom, on both a cultural and sexual level. Forty was considered ancient, an age which seemed ridiculously far away, and one we all hoped we would never reach – to paraphrase The Who.

While of course it was the music of the Beatles that had been the elemental force of this new joyous age, music began to cascade from other bands in England and America too – music which was to push boundaries outward for another thirty years and then become timeless. Young people today are continually rediscovering it. One of my eighteen-year-old sons has an impressive vinyl collection of original albums from the time. Only the other day, he asked me why there are no new guitarists of the calibre of Jimi Hendrix, Eric Clapton, Jimmy Page, George Harrison, and Jeff Beck. I had no answer.

The Beatles' first UK number one had been in 1963; they became international stars with their American tour in 1964, and solidified their legendary status with the release of the studio album *Sgt. Pepper's Lonely Hearts Club Band* in 1967. This opened the way for the canon of concept albums. Life in London was changing breathlessly at breakneck speed, seemingly in tandem with the music.* Popular tastes and culture would never be the same again; English was now the undisputed language of the world.

Tastes in the fields of cinema and theatre were being shaken up commensurately. Male stars with traditional matinee-idol looks were giving way to the spikier personalities of actors such as Michael Caine, Terence Stamp, Albert Finney, Tom Courtenay, and David Hemmings. The girls, while still very beautiful, did not have the classic looks of an Ava Gardner, Grace Kelly, or Rita Hayworth, but exemplified the 'cool' personalities that were emerging.†

* Artists like Bob Dylan, The Beach Boys, The Doors, Jimi Hendrix, and many others in America were making their own spellbinding contributions. English bands were my favourites: The Rolling Stones, The Yardbirds, Cream, The Hollies, The Animals, The Kinks, and The Who, to name only a few.

† Charlotte Rampling, Julie Christie, Susannah York, come immediately to mind, as do the models Jean Shrimpton, Twiggy, and Celia Hammond. Even the establishment figures in photography – e.g. Cecil Beaton, Norman Parkinson – were being joined by a new wave of photographers like David Bailey, Terry O'Neil, Terence Donovan, and Patrick Lichfield, creating a much more casual style whilst becoming a new type of sex symbol themselves. Charlotte Rampling I came to know much later through my friendship with Jeremy Lloyd, to whom she had been briefly engaged early in her career. A wonderful person, talented and as attractive now as she was back then.

The photographs that recorded the lives of the 'beautiful' people who inhabited the clubs, restaurants, and upmarket resorts during the 1960s and '70s were enormously influential. They were the Instagram of their time. Images were as essential to one's social profile then as now – so if the dashing, aristocratic photographer Patrick Lichfield photographed you, you could believe you were 'someone' and that you'd win some column inches the next day.

I never knew him well, but I had met Patrick on many occasions at parties since the early 1970s. He was a great deal of fun to be around; admired for his fabulous photographs as much as for his sense of style, not to mention the beautiful girls always around him, several of whom I also knew.

Diana Vreeland had given Patrick his first big break when she commissioned him to photograph the Duke and Duchess of Windsor in exile in Paris for American *Vogue* in 1966. These images, like many of his photographs, were iconic.

I got to know him better when he settled down in later life with Annunziata Asquith, a great friend of ours, and with whom it was obviously he had found lasting happiness, although tragically this was not to last for as long as we all had hoped.

I remember well a particular conversation with him after dinner one night. Patrick was reminiscing about an old friend of his, the American businessman, and fairly recent Ambassador to Finland, Earle Mack. I'd met Earle briefly a couple of times in New York, but was more familiar with his reputation as a generous and respected businessman who had inherited and then increased a major real estate fortune.

Patrick recalled how he'd been invited to appear on the *Johnny Carson Show*, which was broadcast live, and how Earle Mack had promised him 1,000 dollars if he mentioned his name.

Carson began by introducing Patrick as the famous photographer who just so happened to be a cousin of Queen Elizabeth II and an Earl himself.

'Well, of course,' said Patrick 'here in America you too have an aristocracy.'

'Oh, you mean Hollywood. Well, perhaps, sort of, but it's not the same thing at all. We don't have a Queen of course, and we don't have hereditary titles.'

'Oh, but you do,' Patrick insisted. 'I know several American titles.'

'Like who? What are you talking about?' Carson was puzzled.

'You do have an Earl here. A bona fide American Earl.'

'And who might that be?' Carson asked warily.

'Earle Mack, Earle Mack, Earle Mack, Earle Mack, Earle Mack,' was Patrick's staccato reply before he dissolved into hysterical laughter. Recovering, Patrick explained the name-drop deal to Carson and how Mack now owed him 5,000 dollars. The talk-show host fully appreciated the humour, and I gather that Mack was delighted to settle his debt to Patrick in full.

Dining out in London, apart from a few classic Soho eateries and the grand hotels of the West End, had been a depressing experience for decades, but now fashionable clubs and restaurants sprang up for these new 'beautiful people' to eat, dance, and play in. Before long, their owners and managers became as celebrated as their clientele. Alvaro Maccioni helped kick-start the transformation of London's restaurant scene in a so-called 'Trattoria Revolution', beginning with Trattoria Terrazza in Soho and followed by Alvaro's in the King's Road and La Famiglia at World's End. He co-established the members-only bar / restaurant / disco Club dell'Arethusa in 1967, which prompted Angus McGill in the *Evening Standard* to ask: 'Are you one of the beautiful people? Simple test: Can you get in to the dell'Arethusa?' Alvaro was effectively the godfather of good Italian food in England, and so exclusive did Alvaro's trattoria become apparently, that only 200 people had its ex-directory telephone number.*

---

* 'Alvaro Maccioni – Obituary', the *Daily Telegraph*, 29 November 2013, online: https:// www.telegraph.co.uk/news/obituaries/culture-obituaries/10484998/Alvaro-Maccioni-obituary.html, accessed 22 November 2019.

Mimmo and Lorenzo with their eponymous eateries in Elizabeth Street and Beauchamp Place quickly followed.

I used to be a regular at them all.* Everyone who was anyone danced at Johnny Gold's Tramp and Mark Birley's Annabel's. There were plenty of other places to be seen. Sunday nights – until then an evening when everyone stayed in – took on a special status of its own, as young people returning from a boring weekend with their parents wanted to let off steam. The 'in places' to go were Mr. Chow's in Knightsbridge, Trader Vic's at the London Hilton, and the Hard Rock Café in Piccadilly. Within a few years, The Brasserie on the Fulham Road and Drones on Pont Street had joined the Sunday-evening list.

In stark contrast, I recall the 1950s in images of black and white: the bleakness of post-war rationing, the many abandoned bomb sites, precarious and vacant, others great craters like open wounds throughout central London, mostly serving as temporary car parks, which unconsciously awaited the day of the property developer. There were the cheery-but-filthy coal man with his weekly delivery, the chimney sweep, the grubby rag-and-bone man and his 'rag-and-bone' call, accompanied by the clip-clopping of horse's hooves, the clatter of the cart, and also the tinkers who called door to door willing to do whatever jobs were needed. I remember the tail-end of rationing, the generally drab clothing, the equally drab off-the-shelf furnishings, the smog through which I trudged to school, my mouth covered by a school scarf, and the tiny black and white television set on which I watched children's programmes *Andy Pandy* and the *Sooty Show* starring the aptly-named Sooty and Sweep.

These images were in stark relief to the decade that followed. This way of life was being swept away by the creative noise, humour, and the sheer fun of the 1960s.

Satire, by the likes of David Frost, Peter Cook and Dudley Moore, and the other members of the fringe, was sweeping across the country.

* Often, I saw John Wayne, Sammy Davis Jr., and Frank Sinatra at Alvaro's; Richard Burton and Elizabeth Taylor, and Roger Moore with Tony Curtis at Mimmo's; Sean Connery, George Hamilton, and Eric Clapton at San Lorenzo.

A new wave of 'straight' comedians such as Dave Allen, Tony Hancock, Tommy Cooper, Benny Hill, and the *Carry On* team stoked the hilarity of the nation to the point that the exigencies of high taxes, the devaluation of sterling, and the introduction of exchange controls by Harold Wilson's Labour government were shrugged off.

It is often said that sex did not exist until the Sixties. Witty, but obviously rubbish. What is undeniable, however, is that such an open enjoyment and celebration of sex – whilst surely not original – had not been seen for many decades. The contraceptive pill had of course liberated young women, who seemed as a rule intent on obtaining as much sexual experience as possible before they settled down into the still-traditional roles of wife and mother. Despite their educational advantages – the time of the career woman was fast approaching, but was still a few years away.

Women's Lib was beginning to become a force, but at this point was focused mainly on sexual and educational equality only, as opposed to pay and the workplace.

My first serious female encounter had been with a pretty, buxom, blonde who served us our meals in the school dining room at King's Canterbury. Her name was Christine. She was twenty-six years old to my sixteen. We had become close through my dining alone and late on Saturday evenings because of various fencing competitions in London. I had the slight advantage of wearing 'mufti' (holiday clothes) on those occasions, as opposed to the school uniform of wing collars, white shirts, black ties, black jackets, and pinstriped trousers, which to her must have made my fellow pupils resemble an indistinguishable flock of penguins. Christine used to fuss around me through those late dinners. We graduated to secret meetings once a month at her tiny house in Canterbury.

Morals were indeed lax by today's standards and infidelity before marriage was rife and considered perfectly normal. It seems very strange now, but if a girl accepted an invitation to dinner, there was an automatic and mutual understanding that she would sleep with her date at the end of the evening, unless there had been a terrible row. Everyone had different dates on different evenings, and a good time was had by all.

What a contrast with the behaviour of young people today, who by those standards seem positively straitlaced.

Although I was more than happy to play my part, it was not without its downsides. Among several girlfriends at university, Jennifer was the most serious. She was a long-legged, cool, blonde-haired Sixties beauty, eye catching in her hot pants and miniskirts. I became quite emotionally involved, but after the initial year of a two-year relationship, she began a series of clandestine affairs with a number of my friends. Given the morality of the decade, this was not particularly shocking, but it was hurtful. I became more cynical, warier. Relationship commitment became difficult for me.

Homosexuality was also coming out into the open and fast losing its stigma. The broad mindedness and tolerance of the Sixties would remove its criminality by 1967. The winds of change brought by the Sixties would also sweep away the death penalty for murder in 1965.

I appreciate how fortunate we were as students then compared to those of today. The state paid our university fees and provided a small grant to cover living costs. The cost of living was high for us in those inflationary times, but we all seemed to get by, principally through a large overdraft facility provided by a kindly bank manager. Banks had a very different approach then. University undergraduates were much thinner on the ground, and they were viewed as the high earners of the future. The high-street banks fiercely competed for their accounts, making all forms of credit available to us for indefinite periods. And we, for our part, were happy to take advantage. *Carpe Diem* was after all the creed of the Sixties. Tomorrow could wait, next year was an eternity away.

As the Sixties faded and I left university for law school to become a barrister, the final early girlfriend I should mention was a statuesque, classic blond in the same tutorial class as me with the interesting name of Peta. In fact, Peta was interesting in many ways. She had been educated at Cheltenham Ladies' College and Bristol University, was very bright with a wicked sense of humour, and spent a great deal of time racing at high speed in her yellow MGB sports car from one party to another and from London to Gloucestershire at weekends. With me often in the passenger seat of her open car, we rushed into the early 1970s with enormous enthusiasm.

How Peta managed not only to qualify as a barrister, but also to practise successfully for a few years whilst never out of the social fast lane, I do not know. But she managed it with great style. We remained firm friends. It did not surprise me that in 1980, Peta met and married the charming Adrian Hope, the Earl of Hopetoun (now the 4th Marquess of Linlithgow), with whom she had two children. Sadly, Peta died of tuberculosis in 2009 aged just sixty.

A brilliant light extinguished too soon.

CHAPTER THREE

Moving Swiftly On

C LUTCHING, METAPHORICALLY (I NEVER DID GET AROUND TO collecting it) my 'gentleman's degree', as a third-class honours degree used to be called, I joined the Inner Temple at the Inns of Court, intent on becoming a criminal barrister. I studied for my Bar Exams, kept my 'dining terms' at the Inner Temple, and completed pupillage at 2 Crown Office Row. But the realisation that I would have to spend the next five years in depressing magistrates' courts acting in minor traffic offences for a pittance soon concentrated the mind. By now, many of my school and university friends had well-paying jobs in the City, and I resolved to join them.

At that time, no one, not even a prospective employer, ever asked the class of your degree. They were in short supply, and it was enough that you had one at all, especially from a leading university – at least as far as the City was concerned. Through a contact of my father's, I did a graduate training programme at a small merchant bank called County Bank, and then in 1974 got a good junior position at one with US origins: Manufacturers Hanover Limited.

The Euro-dollar market, from which governments, government agencies, and central banks all over the world obtained an important part of their borrowing, and which is still a critical part of the global financing system, had been created only a few years previously. A market of several trillion US dollars had found its way into the European banking system since the end of the war, and Manufacturers Hanover, Bankers Trust, and S.G. Warburg were the earliest innovators.

This was a specialised business, in which the successful merchant banker needed to have extensive knowledge of the appetite of the world's banks, both for lending to each country's government and the precise interest rate the borrower was prepared to pay and the lender was prepared to accept. A transaction was likely to be in the hundreds of millions of dollars, and the commission a merchant bank would receive would run to several million dollars – significant amounts in those far-off days. Such commissions were rewarded by large bonuses for the successful employee.

It turned out that I had a certain aptitude for this type of banking, and I honed my skills for the next three years, until Bankers Trust International poached me and offered me a quantum leap of both seniority and earnings in 1976. I began to hit my stride. Assisted by luck and timing, I was able to arrange a syndicated loan of 300 million dollars for the Bank of Greece, the first since the fall of the military dictatorship in 1974. I was privileged to work directly with Governor Xenophon Zolotas, later the President of the Hellenic Republic, and our legendary Prime Minister, Constantine Karamanlis. In short order thereafter, I arranged large loans for the Public Power Corporation in Greece, as well as Olympic Airways and the Hellenic Telecommunications Organization (HTO). Then, I raised the largest loan since the end of the war for the Foreign Trade Bank of the Soviet Union. The domino effect of this was getting on the inside track to arrange similar transactions for the central banks of East Germany, Bulgaria, Poland, and Hungary, which I did.

Travelling and doing business behind the Iron Curtain in the mid-1970s was a unique experience. One had an uncomfortable feeling of vulnerability, since the safety of the Western visitor was entirely dependent on the goodwill of his hosts. Most of the time you were received with a grave but faultless courtesy, just as you would expect from high-ranking, educated officials wishing to access the financial markets from which they had been excluded for decades. Whilst my several visits to Moscow were extremely dull – I had been restricted to two or three hard-currency hotels and a similar number of restaurants – I was treated with immaculate consideration. But I was always accompanied by a KGB 'guide', and my sightseeing activities were limited to Red Square, the outside of the Kremlin, and the museum of St. Basil's Cathedral.

In Warsaw and Prague also, I was cordially received – dour, depressing towns though they were then. But I had a truly alarming experience in East Berlin, which I visited every month, entering from West Berlin through Checkpoint Charlie.

The contrast between West and East Berlin was truly remarkable. West Berlin was a colourful, modern, louche, vibrant, highly prosperous city. It represented capitalism at its most successful, its inhabitants busily rushing around making money.

East Berlin was a grey, drab, monolithic expanse of ruins and desolation. It looked unchanged since the Russian occupation began in 1945. Taxis were on average thirty years old and there were few other cars. People were frightened to speak to strangers, constantly under surveillance by the secret police. Everything was regimented, all life dictated by the state. In 1976, the UK government expelled some thirty personnel from the East German Embassy in London on the grounds that they were spies. Retaliation was inevitable.

I was in the wrong place at the wrong time as I sauntered one bright, sunny morning through Checkpoint Charlie into the Eastern Zone on my way to a meeting with the governor of the central bank, nodding cheerily to the heavily armed guards who knew me quite well. To my shock, I was abruptly pulled up to be informed that I was under arrest on the charge of spying for Britain. I was taken below the guard post to a primitive holding room where I was held for two nights, alone except for the occasional visit by a soldier with food. I was not mistreated physically. I received basic meals of bread and soup, but the dread of the unknown and my complete helplessness was overwhelming. Naturally, my many requests for the British Ambassador, the British Consul, and the Greek equivalents, were dismissed out of hand with angry shouts. No one would tell me anything.

It seemed an eternity before I was told I could leave and was offered a ride in a police car to the Hotel Unter den Linden where I normally stayed. Perhaps somewhat rashly I refused this, stating that I had no intention of remaining in the East another ten minutes and that I wanted to cross back to the West through Checkpoint Charlie. The officer in charge simply shrugged and waved me on. It was two in the morning, the weather had turned cold, light snow was falling, and the moon shed little light. I picked my way slowly along the narrow concrete path that wound past barbed wire fences to the Allied Checkpoint. On my approach, three powerful searchlights fixed upon me; through screwed up, squinting eyes I could just make out the soldiers covering me with machine guns in the surrounding gun turrets. I can't think why, but ludicrously I held my British passport up in the air as if it would protect me from the bullets. I was convinced now that this was a set-up, that I would be shot at any moment, and that it would be said afterwards that I was a spy attempting to escape. I remember clearly in those terrified moments that a picture flashed across my mind of Michael Caine playing Harry Palmer in a scene from *The Ipcress File*.

I was enormously relieved to encounter the African American sergeant on duty at the Allied Checkpoint. 'Hey man!' he looked up in surprise, 'Where in hell have you come from?'

Breathlessly, I gestured behind me and presented my crumpled British passport. That night, I checked into the Kempinski Hotel and spent the next few hours getting determinedly drunk before passing out. I swore never to return. And I did not until 2009, twenty years after reunification.

During this '70s period, I was appointed a director of Bankers Trust International at twenty-eight years of age, the youngest of a merchant bank in the City of London. This, together with the high-profile nature of the deals I was putting together, attracted quite a lot of financial press, both in the daily newspapers and those newsletters dedicated to this marketplace. In turn, the gossip columnists – particularly Nigel Dempster of the *Daily Mail* and the William Hickey column of the *Daily Express* – started to latch on to me, chronicling the parties I attended and the girls

I was going out with. I cannot deny that there were many of the latter, and that the publicity helped even more in this respect.

However, I thought rather naïvely that I had arrived socially. As an apparently eligible man about town, the most prestigious clubs and restaurants were delighted to welcome me, and I was showered with invitations to smart dinner parties. But I failed to grasp the transitory nature of flattering publicity: how easily it can turn, be manipulated against you. And we will see a little later how this was accomplished by my first wife, angry ex-girlfriends, and various business associates.

I had also failed to realise that either as a banker or someone managing public companies – as I did for thirty years – your clients and shareholders simply don't want to read about you at all. It makes them nervous. You are supposed to be the wise soul of discretion, not a playboy. I lost track of how many times as a young director my various chairmen used to end an otherwise positive meeting with a small sigh and the remark 'and by the way dear boy, do try and keep out of the press'.

In this era of social media, reality TV, and twenty-four-hour rolling news, it is difficult to understand the importance and influence of the gossip columns of the tabloid newspapers which preceded the internet. This was the only daily medium through which millions of readers were kept abreast of fashions, social events, and the people who attended them. The cast of characters that inhabited these columns had their fifteen minutes of fame bestowed upon them. Many could not cope psychologically when they were abandoned. There was no Facebook and no Instagram to turn to. Newspaper readers often turned straight to the social columns. For many readers, even their actual choice of daily newspaper was dictated by their favourite gossip column. As a result, the columnists wielded great power that was often abused.

In any event, I was now firmly on the road of pursuing my career during the day and my social life under cover of darkness.

CHAPTER FOUR

The Early Working Years

To those of us who were in our early twenties at the time, the first half of the 1970s was very much an extension of the 1960s. And, in fact, both to us and anyone else now studying that period, it is clear that – as regards music, morality, fashion, and the arts – the Sixties really began around 1963/4 and ended in about 1975. A seismic change had taken place, and the Western world then settled into a natural evolution which would take it through to the twenty-first century, with all the subsequent achievements of racial and gender equality, the collapse of communism, higher living standards, longer lifespans, space and supersonic travel, together with a determined assault on poverty and disease everywhere. It would not be until the attack on the World Trade Center on 11 September 2001, and the cataclysmic events that followed, that the huge upswing in terrorism, mass migration of refugees, extremist politics, the return of nationalism, and financial volatility would take hold – presenting us with many of the challenges we face today.*

But in those earlier, carefree times, life continued much as it had, at least for me. As a university student, I had shared a spartan flat with two

---

* This is not the place to begin the serious discussion this statement deserves, but I recall thinking on that day that the world had changed forever, which it has. From a professional perspective (considering that the investment and insurance markets rely on confidence in the global economy to encourage investors to take on long-term risk) confidence was struck a damaging blow from which the world is still recovering.

friends above a pub called the Camden Head off Camden Passage in Islington. This was far from a fashionable area then, but it was definitely 'cool'. The Passage had a crowded antique market every Saturday, and there were two excellent restaurants, Robert Carrier's and Frederick's (not that we could afford them); the Camden Head had live music in the evenings twice a week. At law school, I shared a two-bed mews house with my great friend Raymond Lewis at Weymouth Mews, off Harley Street. That neighbourhood, dominated as it was by private hospitals and doctors' surgeries, was somewhat sterile, to coin a phrase. But the location was excellent for the Inns of Court and for Marylebone High Street, which, with its cheerful pubs and Italian and Greek restaurants, was a short walk away. At our favourite pub, the Baker and Oven, Raymond and I had become so friendly with the Italian staff that we would join their Friday night poker game after closing every week. Since they were all a few years older than us, were working, and our income as students far lower than theirs, the stakes were considerably higher than we could afford – but it was all enormous fun and somehow we muddled through.

It was not long, however, before I too was working, so I qualified for a mortgage. I managed to borrow the deposit as well, and duly bought my first flat in 1973, for the princely sum of 11,700 pounds (around 140,000 pounds now), in Brompton Square, Knightsbridge – just four doors down from our London flat today.

At about this time I was romantically involved with a French girl of my own age called Ghislaine Lejeune. Ghislaine had recently come to London from her native Paris by way of New York. She had been appointed executive editor of English *Vogue*, had a flawless sense of fashion, and bore a remarkable resemblance to a young Marlene Dietrich, even down to the deep, husky voice, albeit with a French not German accent. In addition, she was a descendant of Napoléon Bonaparte through a niece of one of the Emperor's sisters who had married General Baron Lejeune, a favourite general of Napoléon and a leading artist – a fact she loved to dwell upon, often recalling whimsically the irony of a brief affair with Charles Douro, now the Duke of Wellington.

Nevertheless, Ghislaine was a decent sort who was good fun, excellent company, and amused us all in Greece on a couple of visits. For my first trip to New York, she gave me Nan Kempner's telephone number and a letter of introduction.

I had been sent to New York for three months as a trainee by my early employers to attend a banking credit course. I was given a cockroach-infested flat on 3rd Avenue and 55th Street with entirely inadequate air conditioning for the fierce heat of June, July, and August. My salary was low, my subsistence expenses hardly adequate. The saving grace was twofold: first, I made friends with several Americans on the credit course who came from wealthy families, and in that wonderfully hospitable American way, they showered me with weekend invitations to the Hamptons or upstate New York. I was more than happy to escape the grime and heat of 3rd Avenue and took full advantage of these many kindnesses. Second, I did have a few introductions from London.

It is difficult to describe Nan. In these egalitarian days her type is virtually extinct, but as an extremely glamorous fixture of the international social scene, she had achieved iconic status at that time, which is no exaggeration. Her name was synonymous with high fashion. As well known in St. Moritz, the South of France, and London as she was in New York and California, she was loved by designers and aristocrats in equal measure. Her elegance was timeless. Almost forty, but with a glorious figure as slim as any model's, she only wore haute couture and was photographed at every smart party. Nan was the ultimate 'clothes horse'. Valentino, Givenchy, Oscar de la Renta, and Halston were her favourite designers as well as close friends; they often designed their clothes with Nan in mind. Bill Blass and Cardin worshipped her. Always kind and generous, but with an unfailing eye for talent, she was an early supporter of her friend Carolina Herrera.

Nan's Park Avenue apartment was the scene of many sparkling dinners through the years, with celebrated guests from fashion and café society. At lunchtime when in New York, she would hold court at her usual table at Mortimer's restaurant together with her friend Diana Vreeland, the legendary former editor of American *Vogue*.

Nan had been born into a wealthy San Francisco family, was sent to finishing school in Paris, and had grown up a popular, sophisticated fixture of the social scene on the West and East Coasts of America. As expected, she had married appropriately well. Tommy Kempner was the nephew of John Loeb, the head of Loeb, Rhoades & Co., and a titan of Wall Street. John Loeb himself had married a Lehman, thereby cementing links between two great Jewish investment-banking families. Loeb, Rhodes & Co. was a financial powerhouse that arranged and underwrote the new debt issues of many of the largest companies in America. Tommy was a partner of the firm.

Nan and Tommy had two sons – both destined to become successful financiers – but after several years, the marriage was in trouble. The problem was that whilst Tommy had few interests outside business and golf, Nan was immersed in fashion and parties, quoted as saying she 'would go to the opening of a door'. Parties and openings bored Tommy, and a tacit agreement that each would discreetly lead their own life was reached. Nevertheless, at the time I met Nan, Tommy was having a much too public affair with an old friend of them both, to the fury of Nan.

I was unaware of much of this, but I was not so innocent that I did not realise Nan's kindness to a visitor to New York was not entirely platonically extended. I was, though, slightly surprised that she made no attempt to hide both her initial interest in me and then our subsequent relationship. This spanned about a year and embraced, during my breaks from the office, London, New York, Paris, Los Angeles, Mexico, the Bahamas, and Greece. Still in my early twenties, this was indeed a formative relationship through which I met a great number of well-known, talented people.

Self-evidently, Nan was both married and older than I was – although still very beautiful. I was beginning to realise that I was, at this point, physically attracted to women who were more mature than I. In fact, throughout most of my life, I have found that the age I find a beautiful woman most attractive is somewhere from just under thirty to just over forty. The combination of glamour and sophistication, with striking looks was always irresistible to me. Even now, although I can appreciate younger women aesthetically, I am not drawn to them. Ghislaine, strangely enough, always seemed resentful, jealous even, of the affair with Nan which she herself had initiated. Why I am not sure, particularly since she was always drawn to distinguished older men, leaving me, for example, for a well-known journalist called Derek Hart.

In any event, for the time being the relationship with Nan went careering headlong, full steam ahead. We flew around the world from party to opening to fashion show to holidays in the sun. Nan introduced me to the Lyford Cay Club in Nassau, the capital of the Bahamas, which had recently been built on land reclaimed from marshland by the sea. I had first visited Nassau as a guest at Graycliff, having been invited by my friend from law school, Prince John Radziwiłł. The house then belonged to his mother's second husband, Eric, Earl of Dudley. This imposing mansion was opposite Government House, where Wallis, Duchess of Windsor had spent the war years. It is now a gloomy, but grand, hotel.

Lyford, at the other end of the island, was so much more amusing. There I met Bill Paley, the founder of CBS, and Neil McConnell, an Avon heir, who were both building houses within the compound. I played cards with Arnaud de Borchgrave, foreign news editor of *Time* magazine, Henryk de Kwiatkowski, a leading aircraft dealer, and Spyros Skouras, head of 20th Century Fox.* It was all enormous fun. Lyford has been an annual winter escape to the sun for me ever since, thanks entirely to the generous hospitality of Anthony and Kathryn Klonaris. Both of whose families originated from Kalymnos, having been sent to the Bahamas for the sponge industry by my uncle Nikos Vouvalis. Anthony was at law school with John Radziwiłł and me. It's a small world indeed.

---

* I also met John Menzies, owner of the eponymous bookshops, his great character of a brother-in-law, Sir Trevor Dawson, and Shirley Oakes, the daughter of the mysteriously murdered Canadian real estate millionaire Sir Harry Oakes.

∽

Back to New York and the banking credit course, and one evening Nan took me to Drue Heinz's house in Sutton Square for dinner. Drue, English originally, was a renowned hostess, recently widowed from Jack Heinz of the canned-food family. There were twenty-four guests that night, arranged on four tables, and I was quite bowled over to find myself sitting opposite Sir Alec Guinness, an actor I had much admired since childhood. He could not have been more gracious to me, nor more pleasant to everyone around him. I asked him several questions about his work which he must have been asked a hundred times before, but he had no hesitation in answering with great charm and self-deprecating humour.

It turned out that Sir Alec was in New York to help promote the John le Carré television adaptation of *Tinker Tailor Soldier Spy*, which I had watched avidly in England a few months previously. When I ventured how much I had enjoyed the series, he replied wryly that he was dreading the American opening. Apparently, so few English reviewers had followed the complexities of the plot, that he was convinced even fewer American critics would grasp it.

I am deeply embarrassed to recount that when he complimented me on the tie I was wearing, I had drunk enough to immediately remove it and press it upon him. I babbled some star-struck nonsense to the effect that he must accept the tie if it would give him half the pleasure his performances had given me! From a distance of forty-five years, I am still mortified by this crass behaviour. However, such was the mark of the man that not only did he accept the tie with good grace, but the following took place the next morning.

It was around eleven o'clock. I was sitting at my desk in the open-plan office for the thirty attendees of the credit course. There was one bored female secretary in the front corner who fielded the few incoming calls we received.

The phone rang. 'Mr. Olympitis,' she called out, 'Sir Alec Guinness, line three.'

A hush went around the 'bull pit'. My stomach turned over with excitement.

'Hallo, hallo,' I mumbled.

'Manoli, my dear boy, I hope I haven't disturbed you,' the great man said, 'I got your number from Drue. I just had to call and thank you so much for that awfully kind gesture of yours, giving me that lovely tie. Thank you again, you really shouldn't have.'

Extremely conscious of the others, my voice not only strengthened but now also took on a tone of unwarranted familiarity.

'It was my pleasure Alec, any time at all. I hope we can have lunch sometime soon.'

My stock soared with all my classmates for the remainder of my time in New York. I am quite sure he made the call for just that reason. Unfortunately, I never had the chance to meet him again, except by chance in a butcher's shop on Elizabeth Street in London many years later. He pretended to remember me of course, which I very much doubted. But one thing I am sure of is that, when he made the *Tinker Tailor* sequel series, *Smiley's People*, Alec Guinness wore the tie I gave him in the very first episode. That was no coincidence. A great gentleman, it was his way of showing me how much he really liked it.

In London again, one Friday in the spring of 1976, Nan suggested we go to an open-air Rolling Stones concert at Knebworth the following day. She had a friend called Ahmet Ertegun, the co-founder of Atlantic Records. He was close to the Stones, having had them briefly under contract, and was currently in London. We joined him and our mutual friend David Metcalfe for lunch at San Lorenzo with the result that Ahmet invited us as his guests to come backstage to watch the concert.

I hurried to hire a car and driver, and, as arranged, we joined Ahmet's convoy of cars to the Knebworth Estate at noon on Saturday – our modest saloon followed by two stunning brunette models in a red Mercedes sports car. They had got wind of this the previous day in San Lorenzo and tagged along.

I have to admit to a star-struck afternoon. Ahmet was treated like the record king he was by security guards, artists, and guests alike. Not only were the Rolling Stones on top form, but backstage afterwards they were charming and convivial, Marianne Faithfull and Anita Pallenberg drifting around them. Jack Nicholson was there with the young Paul Getty, recently released from his kidnapping ordeal and minus one ear. Jack seemed to be enjoying himself, but the Getty boy was unsurprisingly melancholy and reflective. Several minor British pop stars were milling about after the show trying to make an impression, but as we all seated ourselves at the trestle tables laid out for supper, the highlight of my evening was the arrival of Paul McCartney, which impressed me enormously. He entered jauntily, unannounced and alone, dressed in sneakers, a white T-shirt, leather jacket, and blue jeans. Practically unnoticed, but waving to Ahmet and Mick Jagger, he sat down modestly in the midst of the session musicians at their end of the table and immediately joined in their banter, mainly anecdotes of past tours and recording sessions. Probably the biggest music star on the planet, but at heart one of their own.

It was through Nan also that I became friends with Mark Birley, the stylish founder of Annabel's. For this too, I was grateful.

I had become a junior member of this legendary nightclub while still a student in 1970. Entrance to that magical world, filled with style and celebrated faces, virtually guaranteed a successful night with the vast majority of desirable single girls. But to an impecunious student, dinner there was financially out of reach. However, my friends and I had invented a winning formula. When asking a beautiful girl out to dinner, we would casually let Annabel's slip as a possible venue. This would make a definite impression as letting the girl know you were a member firmly established your credentials. A day or so later, one would then apologetically excuse oneself from actual dinner on the basis of a last-minute parental engagement or something similar, but suggest drinks and breakfast instead – which began at Annabel's at eleven o'clock. This would invariably be accepted with alacrity. It was still Annabel's, and around midnight was the most exciting time to be there in any case. A glass or two of champagne, followed by an excellent full English breakfast was much cheaper than dinner. Affordable, and just as effective. It would compensate for hiding hungrily at home between seven and eleven in the evening.

I had met Mark briefly in the club. He would nod approvingly at me, since I was often accompanied by particularly pretty girls. Nan and he were very close. Several of Nan's girl friends had been romantically involved with Mark; they were both a significant part of the same international set. He and I got on famously together, he was mildly amused by my early adventures at Annabel's. Then, one weekend the three of us, together with a girlfriend of Mark's, spent a weekend at the Bas-Bréau inn in Barbizon, by Versailles. This would be my first experience of Mark's expansive approach to shopping. He scoured the local antique shops, harvesting treasure after treasure for both Annabel's and his soon-to-be-opened new club, Marks. This was followed by a visit to a neighbouring men's clothes shop. I admit to being quite intimidated by Mark's habit of buying several dozen identical silk shirts at a time if he came across one that he especially liked. This extended to ties, socks, virtually any item of clothing. It made my purchase of two Hermès ties look slightly pathetic.

Nevertheless, the weekend was a great success. Mark and I remained friends for the rest of his life. He was kind enough to make me a founder member of not only Mark's Club, but also Harry's Bar and George in later years. These uniquely English establishments all provided a luxurious backdrop to the various phases of my own life. I took over Harry's Bar, for example, to celebrate my son John's christening soon after it opened. I dined at Mark's Club at least twice a week for two decades, and I gave my fortieth birthday party there. I had more marvellous times in Annabel's, Mark's, and Harry's Bar than I can possibly remember.

Mark's impeccable taste (inherited no doubt from his father, the renowned royal portrait painter Sir Oswald Birley), his exquisite attention to detail, his perfectionism have never been remotely equalled by the creator of any other London private members club – and I am certain won't be, in my lifetime anyway. It was not for nothing that the most famous people on Earth, from every walk of life, would join or visit. Mark Birley was an original.

Time after time, Mark would turn down highly attractive offers to open branches of his clubs in foreign towns. He always told me this would be a certain recipe for disaster. Mark ascribed the success of his restaurants to the fact that he would personally eat lunch or dinner, or drop in for a drink every single day at each one, tirelessly demanding perfection from his loyal, superb staff in every detail. He was convinced that without his constant presence, standards would slip. He could not bear this thought, even though his son, Robin, would have been more than equal to the task. Shortly before his death, Mark sold all his clubs. It really was the end of an era.

CHAPTER FIVE

On My Way

I N 1976, I SOLD BROMPTON SQUARE FOR A PROFIT OF OVER 10,000 pounds, which seemed a fortune to me, and I joined Bankers Trust International. The latter for a much higher salary and a senior middle management role, the former because my good friend Laurie Hunter had also sold his flat for a decent profit, and since we had the same circle of pals and girlfriends, we thought it would be fun to share a house for a while. We found a gaily painted, two-bedroom cottage in Godfrey Street, just off Chelsea Green. This house became 'party central', permanently full of pretty girls, champagne, and hysterical laughter. It was also of great help that the newest, most fashionable disco club, Wedgies, had opened on the King's Road around the corner. Laurie and I had a prime table reserved for every weeknight. Whichever girls we did not take there for dinner, could usually be persuaded to come for drinks and dancing afterwards. From there, it was a short hop home.

All this, together with a decent income (and now a bit of capital), provided me with the happiest, most carefree, and completely exuberant times of my bachelor life. Although, difficult to believe perhaps, I was working extremely hard at my career at the same time. That seemed to be going well too.

I was even finding time to play poker for quite high stakes. At this I was successful, but I predictably squandered most of the profits in my visits to the Clermont Club and Aspinalls, where I was playing casino games against the House. Nevertheless, on balance, in gambling too I was ahead.

I played poker every Saturday night at the house of Larry Collins, a well-known American writer, and Nadia, his charismatic Egyptian born wife. These were agreeable games with nice people.* Larry had been a journalist on *Newsweek* before turning author, and interesting journalistic friends passing through London would often turn up to play. John Chancellor, the NBC news anchor, and Pierre Salinger, Jack Kennedy's Press Secretary at the White House, were regular attendees. Pierre was especially welcome. He was a huge personality who loved to tell fascinating stories of his time in Washington whilst making extravagant bets, which he usually lost.

This reminds me of a story about Larry Collins that always amused me. While at *Newsweek* in Paris in the early 1960s, he and his writing partner Dominique Lapierre wrote their bestselling first book, *Is Paris Burning?* They received a call from Darryl Zanuck unexpectedly. The founder of 20th Century Fox, now an independent producer, he had just produced the extremely successful war film *The Longest Day*, and wanted to buy the film rights to their book. He arranged to take them to lunch at The Ritz Hotel in two weeks' time.

Most excited by this, the fledgling writers turned to their mentor, the novelist Irwin Shaw, for advice. Irwin urged them not to speak to Zanuck without an agent, and he introduced them to his – the celebrated Swifty Lazar.

'Kids,' said Swifty, a diminutive figure with an imposing attitude and a tough, no-nonsense voice, 'I'll fly over and join you for the lunch. Let me do the talking. Don't say a word.'

---

* Our regular group included my best friend from law school, now a criminal barrister, Raymond Lewis; two charming Egyptian banker friends of Nadia who lived in London; Forbes Singer, an American businessman; Baron Teddy van Zuylen, a scion of Royal Dutch Shell; and Dan Meinertzhagen, a professional gambler from an English establishment family who was a long-standing friend of us all.

On the appointed day, the three of them were at the restaurant table, awaiting Darryl Zanuck's arrival. He entered. Another diminutive figure, with a huge cigar clamped between his teeth.

'Oh, hello Swifty,' he growled and sat down, not best pleased.

'Good trip, Zanuck?' Swifty did not draw breath, 'These are my boys. I speak for them. So settle the deal now. Then we eat.'

Zanuck nodded resignedly.

'What's your offer?' Swifty asked.

'250,000 dollars.'

Larry and Dominique almost passed out. A sum beyond their wildest dreams.

'You are kidding,' Swifty shot back.

'500,000 dollars. Nothing less.'

The authors exchanged alarmed glances.

Zanuck sighed. He held his cigar, staring at it for a while before answering.

'I wish you hadn't come all this way, Swifty. I really do. Nothing personal; 250 grand or zero. That's the deal. Take it or leave it.'

'Then we'll leave it.' Swifty gestured to Larry and Dominique to be quiet.

'Okay,' Zanuck sighed again and stood up, 'lunch is still on me, order what you like. Nice to meet you, boys. See you around, Swifty.' He left.

'Relax. There's no problem,' Swifty reassured his shell-shocked clients.

'I've dealt with Zanuck for years. It's all bullshit. He's a great actor. Better than all the ones he's employed. He'll be back. I guarantee it.'

They never heard from Zanuck again. Eventually, the rights were sold to a lesser filmmaker for not even 100,000 dollars. The film flopped, albeit with a talented cast. But they did go on to write *Freedom at Midnight*, *O Jerusalem!*, *Or I'll Dress You in Mourning*, and many other bestsellers together, with Swifty Lazar still as their agent for the next twenty years, until he died.

I can't, however, say that all my times playing poker with Larry are remembered as fondly as the intimate evenings at his and Nadia's. A particular poker game in the mid-1970s remains the source of some embarrassment to me.

Separately, Larry and I received telephone calls from a controversial, down-on-her-luck society hostess, about a poker game she was organising on behalf of two Italian industrialist sisters visiting London. They had rented a grand house full of staff in Hill Street, not far from the Dorchester Hotel. We both accepted and duly turned up together in the early evening on the appointed day. The sisters were charming; the three other players were London-based Italians whom neither Larry nor I knew, but they were equally charming and clearly equally wealthy. None of them were skilful poker players, but they obviously enjoyed gambling, didn't much care about losing, and consequently the stakes were relatively high. By the time we took a break for a buffet dinner, Larry and I were each between two or three thousand pounds ahead.

The Greek billionaire Philip Niarchos arrived halfway through dinner with an erudite, serious, middle aged Saudi Prince, dressed impeccably in a Savile Row suit. I knew Philip quite well, but had never met the Saudi, although Larry knew of him and informed me he was a respected diplomat.

As I expected, Philip left when the game was about to resume, gambling bored him; the Saudi, however, remained. He then not only asked if he could join in, but whether there would be any objections to changing the game from poker to chemin de fer, which was apparently his favourite. The Italians agreed enthusiastically. That left Larry and me in a difficult position. We were winning, we could hardly refuse to play, demand to be paid, and leave, and yet we were both well aware that chemin de fer is a game in which the stakes can become astronomical when played by wealthy risk-takers. So, to cut our downside as much as possible we agreed to play together, taking one seat at the table, with me playing the hand and Larry sitting behind me. Moreover, as the stakes indeed began to escalate, we resorted to the option of only covering a part of the bank's wager when it became our turn.

The main reason the stakes were increasing was that our newfound Saudi friend was losing heavily, and his mood was darkening rapidly. In the end, he was virtually the only loser. The big winner was one of the Italian men, but our luck had held, and Larry and I had increased our own winnings threefold. Larry was already successful, but my share was a fortune to me. It would easily clear my bank overdraft as well as make serious inroads into my mortgage. The Saudi had his driver take the relevant details and announced grumpily that we would all be paid during banking hours the following day. I went home and hardly slept the rest of the night, high on nerves and excitement.

Imagine then my extreme disappointment, swiftly turning to rage, when the hostess that had organised the game, together with a well-known Lebanese middleman who looked after rich Arabs in London, telephoned everyone to inform them that the Saudi had decided not to pay. They were most apologetic, they had tried to obtain payment for everyone, but had failed. They did not know the reason. In a fury, I managed to reach Philip Niarchos who was surprised, but understandably did not wish to get involved, his father was doing business with the Saudi royal family.

And there the matter would have ended, had I not been a guest on Sam Spiegel's yacht one night nearly ten years later. As I came on board for drinks before dinner, Sam was introducing his guests to each other, and I found myself shaking hands with the Saudi from that night. He did not remember me. Anger welled up inside me, and, raising my voice, I accused him of not paying his gambling debts, reminding him of his appalling behaviour. He was shocked, outraged, and indignant.

'You are rude, you are mad, you are a liar!' he shouted.

'Is this young man a bad joke?' he turned to a horrified Sam.

'I paid every penny, my people sent over every penny, in cash, cash!' He was shaking with rage. 'We paid before 11 o'clock, I said 11 o'clock! The very next morning! I demand an apology immediately!'

It suddenly all became clear to me. I wished the deck could somehow eject me into the sea. I was truly mortified. How stupid I had been. I apologised on the spot and excused myself with deep humility. Of course he had paid. Why wouldn't he have done? The hostess and the Lebanese fixer had taken all the money for themselves. It was so obvious now. The Saudi prince graciously accepted my explanation. But I am still incredibly embarrassed at the recollection of this unfortunate event.

I was also often playing punto banco/baccarat* at the Clermont Club in a regular group that included the Shah of Persia's ambassador of the day, Mohammed Reza Armiteymour. A most elegant and charming gentleman, whose beautiful daughter, Roya, would often sit behind him during the game. We became quite friendly, but nothing more. One New Year's Eve at Wedgies, Roya invited me to join her table for a drink, and I introduced her to Laurie. Within months, I was hosting an engagement party for them, and a few months later, they were married. My most vivid memory of that wedding was the attendance of film legend Ava Gardner who was a close friend and neighbour of Roya's aunt. A goddess, perhaps not as young but as beautiful as ever, and clearly still up for a late night, she came on to Tramp after dinner with Laurie, Roya, our friend Forbes Singer, and me. In rather an unreal, unforgettable couple of hours, we all danced together until the early hours of the following morning. I was of course extremely happy for Laurie and Roya, but sorry to see Laurie leave to begin married life. However, I soldiered on bravely, alone at Godfrey Street, doing my best to make up for his absence to as many girls as I could.

My work life in the meantime had now really taken off, and age twenty-eight I was appointed to the board, the City of London's youngest director of a merchant bank, now earning an even higher salary. I was travelling a great deal on business, first class now, staying in the best hotels in the world, on a generous expense account.

This lifestyle, the prominent friends that I had made along the way, together with increasing press exposure was heightening my social

---

* As a casino game in Asia, the US, and the UK, the variation baccarat/punto banco displaced the classic French game chemin de fer in the late 1950s. The latter is still played in a few European and Latin American casinos. The main difference between the two is that players of baccarat/punto banco bet against the bank, in chemin der fer they bet against each other.

reputation considerably. And so it was that I began a relationship with Tessa Dahl, the beautiful actress, model, and 'it girl' of the day.

Tessa's father was the celebrated children's author Roald Dahl, her mother the Oscar-winning actress Patricia Neal. Today, Tessa is perhaps known mainly as the mother of the former supermodel Sophie Dahl, but then, she was a renowned twenty-four-year-old beauty who had just appeared in Roman Polanski's film *Dance of the Vampires* and had a series of high-profile affairs behind her. One of these, with the actor Julian Holloway, resulted in Sophie. She was about three years of age when I first met Tessa, and was an enchanting child. I dutifully took her to present a bouquet of flowers to the Queen Mother on some occasion that I cannot now recall. She pulled it off beautifully.

Tessa and I had an amusing albeit brief time together. We have stayed friends ever since, through two of her marriages, only one of mine – you'll understand why later – and several relationships each. She moved from London a few years ago, and now lives in Martha's Vineyard to where her mother had retired.

Patricia Neal, Tessa's mother, was a Hollywood star of the first magnitude. A wonderful, vivacious, popular actress, she had illuminated many films before she won her Best Actress Oscar opposite Paul Newman in *Hud*. Some time prior to that, she had fallen deeply in love with Gary Cooper, with whom she had starred in *The Fountainhead*. He promised he would leave his wife Rocky to marry her. It was her tragedy that 'Coop' got cold feet, sending her instead the hollow parting gift of a fur coat. Patricia married Roald Dahl on the rebound, but never got over Gary Cooper. Early into her marriage to Roald, she suffered a debilitating stroke from which, mainly as a result of her husband's ingenious inventions of physiotherapy equipment, she made an astonishing recovery. However, thereafter one or two drinks would go straight to her head with the result that, to Roald's irritation, she frequently reminisced aloud about Gary Cooper, until long after Cooper's death. One Boxing Day evening, the four of us, Patricia, Tessa, Roald, and I, were dining together at the Curzon House Club when Patricia started to reminisce in this vein.

The reason for my presence on this particular evening was that Roald had taken a shine to me, because he perceived that I had both a high profile and a secure job, unlike all of Tessa's previous boyfriends. When Tessa announced that her father wanted to take us to 'his club' on Boxing Day night, I must admit I wondered which club could be open over the Christmas holidays, and then realised it must be a casino and thus, in all likelihood, a complementary dinner for him and his guests.

The restaurant was packed for the free dinner, full mainly of the club's more boisterous Jewish members and their families, to whom Christmas was by definition not an important holiday. Although they represented many of the club's regular punters, this was not a crowd that naturally endeared itself to Roald Dahl's frankly bigoted nature. And Patricia's Gary Cooper stories were getting on his nerves again. Dinner for us was a fraught affair, with poor Tessa becoming increasingly nervous of her father's black mood and irritated by her mother's ramblings. I tried to make banal conversation as best I could to no effect, other than to annoy Tessa even more.

Over coffee, Roald stood up abruptly and stalked from our table to the fireplace in the centre of the ornate dining room. A tall, striking man, he held up his wine glass, tapping it with a knife, demanding silence. A hush fell, the other guests proudly pointing out their celebrated fellow member to their wives.

'Good evening,' his face was impassive, 'I should like to say a few words.'

The crowd, still proud, clapped and cheered at length. 'Hooray for Roald!'

'I should like simply to say' he continued, 'how standards are indeed slipping at this club.'

Many of the guests had not heard him above the din. Oblivious of his remarks, they cheered again. Aghast, Tessa tried to persuade her father back to the table in vain.

'The food tonight was inedible,' silence fell, 'the wine undrinkable, and the people here are indescribably ghastly. And so, I drink to you all with this revolting wine.'

There was a low murmuring. Roald lifted his glass mockingly to the room.

He returned to his wife. She had noticed nothing out of the ordinary, and was still droning on. He poured himself more wine and sat back in his chair more content, more relaxed than he had been all evening. Tessa had her head in her hands. I was dumbfounded.

A few moments later, the manager and two security guards came to our table to tell us that we were no longer welcome, that they would like us to leave immediately. Tessa jumped up, as did I, Patricia smiled vaguely, and Roald refused point-blank to move.

'Certainly not. I'm going to play blackjack upstairs.'

'You don't seem to understand,' the manager said tersely, 'you, none of you, are welcome here. Ever again. Get out.'

'Please Daddy,' Tessa begged, 'let's go.'

As her father shook his head obstinately, I interjected that I would take them as my guests to a casino around the corner called The Hertford Club. We could play blackjack and have a nightcap there.

Roald reluctantly agreed. Tessa smiled gratefully at me for the first time that evening, and that's what we did.

The evening ended on a better note since both Roald and I had a lucky run at the blackjack table. He went home in an excellent mood. A mood that was not even marred by an unfortunate piece written by Nigel Dempster in his Diary Column two days later chronicling the whole embarrassing story, clearly based on a leak from the Curzon House Club. In fact, Roald began to believe I was lucky for him at blackjack. For some years afterwards he would telephone me out of the blue to tell me he was playing and demand that I should join him, which I occasionally did. We were quite friendly by now; however, much later, he let me down on the one occasion he could have helped me, as we shall see. A gifted writer, but a cold, unpleasant man.

Cold and unpleasant were definitely not words that could ever be attributed to Ira von Fürstenberg. She was, and still is, one of the nicest, kindest people I have ever known. It was my good fortune to meet her at the house of our mutual friend, designer Mimmi O'Connell, towards the end of 1978, when I was close to thirty.

Ira is an Agnelli on her mother's side (of the Fiat family), the daughter of an Austrian prince, Tassilo zu Fürstenberg, on the other. Born therefore a truly beautiful princess as well as an industrial heiress, she first made headlines by eloping and marrying at fifteen years of age the considerably older Prince Alfonso von Hohenlohe, creator of the Marbella Club. This scandal shocked the society of the 1950s. Although the marriage produced two sons, it did not last. Ira then lived for three years with the Brazilian playboy Francisco 'Baby' Pignatari, before pursuing a career as a film actress in Italy and then a fashion-oriented businesswoman. A universally popular, life-enhancing person, she was invited everywhere.

It was my even better good fortune to begin a close relationship with her that I recall with immense affection. Ira based herself at Godfrey Street for a time, whilst commuting to various business-related events in Madrid, Rome, Milan, and Paris. Half our time together was quite grand. She would take me to impossibly smart evenings at the houses of her friends, such as Heini Thyssen, the German industrialist, a very close friend of Princess Margaret; Roberto Campos, the Brazilian ambassador; and the publisher Lord George Weidenfeld. I would take her to our mutual friend David Metcalfe's, to Mark's Club, Harry's Bar, Annabel's, and home to Greece. I'm afraid I ruined our highly agreeable life together by getting carried away and asking her to marry me. Ira was not in the mood to settle down, and I realised that I had insufficient funds to maintain her lifestyle in any case. Somewhat wistfully, and gently, she could not accept. And to make matters worse, she then left me and disappeared with an impecunious Swiss ski instructor.

Little was I to know then what further adventures life had in store for us a little way down the road, but at that point I was depressed and dejected, and it was in that irrational state of mind that I met my first wife on a business trip to New York.

That's my excuse anyway.

CHAPTER SIX

Enter Jan Cushing

I N LATE SUMMER OF 1979, I WAS STAYING AT THE REGENCY HOTEL on Park Avenue in New York. My schedule was for two nights, and I was looking forward to a date on the second night with a pretty, young, petite English brunette by the name of Susan Alderton. She had moved to the United States from our London office where she had been involved with a colleague and thus up to this point 'off limits', but she was now seemingly keen to extend her romantic boundaries. I often wonder how different my future would have been had I kept that date with Susan. On such small moments can our lives turn.

I spent the first day in meetings with my New York team, debriefing them of our Greek transactions and sharing strategy for a tour of Eastern European capitals to begin in October. Tired and jet lagged, I called John Radziwiłł on my return to the hotel. John now resided around the corner at 834 5th Avenue with his recent wife, Greek shipowner's daughter Eugenia Carras, and, although I was planning an early night with room service, I allowed myself to be persuaded to walk over for dinner a little later. And so it happened that I met Jan Cushing that fateful evening.

My first (and entirely inaccurate) impression of her was of a beautiful, but nervous and fragile, blonde fawn. Her green eyes constantly darted around the dining room from under a mane of long blonde hair. Her head moved in unison with her eyes, her nostrils slightly flared as if attuned to the scent of ever-present danger. Her conversation, while often witty and sometimes quite spiteful, jumped erratically from one topic to another. The effect was that I found her entertaining yet vulnerable. And all the while she would pepper you with direct, indiscreet questions.

In fact, there was nothing nervous or fearful about Jan that had not been induced by a combination of prescription drugs and alcohol. She was the reverse of fragile. The words of Norman Mailer later rang in my ears: 'a born killer, she takes no prisoners'. But she was a brilliant natural actress who fooled far cleverer people than me. Jan excelled as a hostess. She entertained generously and continually, her Madison Avenue and 79th Street apartment was a throwback to those classic salons frequented by literary and political figures. Accordingly, she counted illustrious statesmen, businessmen, writers, actors, and directors amongst her closest friends.

There was, however, a significant insecurity underlying her highly-strung, brittle personality. Stimulants would enhance this to produce sudden, unpredictable mood swings. One moment Jan could be amusing, generous, and attractive, a split second later she could become aggressive and vindictive. As such, she was entirely closed to reason. Green eyes blazing, she would mercilessly berate anyone she imagined had insulted or criticised her. I have often wondered whether today she might be diagnosed as bipolar, but then this condition was unknown – and in New York in particular, the possession of a great deal of money can usually compensate for the most appalling behaviour. To Jan's many acolytes, socially and amongst the press, her dreadful behaviour invariably translated into an amusing anecdote.

I believe that Jan's insecurity stemmed from a strong anti-Semitism that was tragic in one who had been born into an extremely wealthy Jewish family. Without question, Jan was the most anti-Semitic person I have ever met. Her striking blonde looks belied the fact that she was Jewish. The circles to which she aspired were innately anti-Semitic, so Jan stridently adopted their prejudices to gain acceptance to the highest echelons of New York society.

However, Jan was proud of her Jewish grandfather. Samuel Golding, a legendary real estate and banking mogul, had immigrated to New York with his parents in the 1920s from Russia, soon after the Revolution. He could have been a character from a novel. An illiterate, penniless teenager, Sam sold flypaper on the city streets. From such humble beginnings, he would found a real estate empire that included much of the borough of Queens, large tracts of midtown Park Avenue (including the land under the Regency Hotel), and build the Essex House, an imposing residential building close to the Plaza Hotel off 5th Avenue, overlooking Central Park. He founded the Sterling National Bank, of which he was chairman and which he would later sell to the Bank of New York for another fortune shortly before his death in 1975.

Sam Golding's two sons were in the business. Both of them died before him of heart attacks brought on, according to Jan's strangely gleeful account to me of her own father's death, by overwork. Each son had left behind an infant daughter, and the two cousins were the sole and joint beneficiaries of the Golding Trusts. These trusts had a net worth of nearly 100 million dollars.

Jan's father, Arnold Golding, she therefore never knew. He had died when she was three months old. Her mother Bernice, a charming, well-educated lady, Jan intensely disliked for no obvious reason other than she had not attained Jan's social heights. Her stepfather, a quietly spoken, generous man was called Billy Rose. Billy made a great deal of money in the textile business, was part owner of the Yankees baseball team, and a high-stakes gambling companion of many famous entertainers. Ashamed of Billy's Jewish looks and his lack of formal education, Jan disliked him too.

None of Jan's complex nature was apparent to me until much later. All I saw that first night was a famously beautiful, witty, New York society hostess of about my own age whom I found extremely attractive, and who, at the end of the evening, asked me to join a dinner party the following night which she was giving at her apartment. An invitation I accepted enthusiastically and which led to my cancelling plans with Susan.

There was no dinner party the following night. I entered her splendid apartment next to the Carlyle Hotel, was ushered into an impressive sitting room by a Colombian housekeeper, given a glass of champagne, and could see a table laid for two in the candlelit dining room across the mahogany-floored hallway. A favourite gambit, as I later discovered, but one that amused me at the time.

It must be painfully obvious by now to any reader that I was out of my depth. Jan looked ravishing that night, a picture of poise and sophistication, perfectly heightened by the glorious, framed photographs of her on the covers of American *Vogue* and *Harper's Bazaar* that hung amongst the paintings on the dining room wall. I extended my stay in New York by a week, and she travelled back to London with me, taking up residence in Godfrey Street. A month later, we moved to a spacious flat in Rutland Gate, and a month after that we decided to get married – thus proving the adage 'marry in haste, repent at leisure'.

Without question, I was dazzled by the superficial qualities of Jan, to the point that my judgment was non-existent. I cannot even plead the normal defence of being blinded by love, for although I thought I was, I now know much better. I was bowled over by her looks and her charisma and, regrettably, by her lifestyle and her famous friends. Even the fact that I was husband number three did not give me pause for thought. It was completely ridiculous of me.

Jan's first husband was Del Coleman, a charming and entertaining man, but allegedly a Wall Street front for significant gambling interests of some of the Chicago and New York Mafia families. His company, Parvin Dorman, controlled slot machines and casinos in Las Vegas amongst other investments. Jan had been nineteen to his forty-two when she married him. Del's best man had been Sidney Korshak, rumoured to be the most powerful man in organised crime in America. Legend had it that as a young lawyer in Chicago, Korshak advised Al Capone in the 1920s and he subsequently advised the leading Mafia families in Chicago. Certainly, he was now the long-time senior legal counsel to the Teamsters' Union. The latter pension fund had financed much of the early Las Vegas. Jan's marriage to Del was annulled after a few months, but she remained on close terms with them both. These well-known friendships gave the more extreme physical threats that Jan often made in the heat of an alcohol-fuelled tirade a certain ring of legitimacy, creating fear amongst her enemies.

Freddie Cushing was the second husband. A member of a prominent Newport, Rhode Island, Social-Register family, Freddie was tall, blonde, good looking, charming, and welcome everywhere. With this marriage, Jan Cushing had smashed the Jewish glass ceiling and arrived socially. It gave her the platform to establish herself as hostess to the distinguished, gifted, and famous. Her wealth alone could not have achieved it, but combined with her new aristocratic name, her beauty, and an outrageously amusing persona, the package was an irresistible draw. To top all that, the faux glamour of the supposed Mafia connection added a dash of notoriety to the heady cocktail.

This marriage lasted seven years. The amiable Freddie was not the brightest individual, but he had managed to graduate from Harvard and was employed by Lehman Brothers in Paris as a private banker, earning a minimal salary but with the luxury of a wealthy wife. Thus, it was in Paris that Jan launched herself as the hostess to politicians, writers, artists in general, and tycoons.

At this stage, the arrival of Henry Kissinger, recently appointed by President Richard Nixon as Secretary of State, to conduct the Vietnam peace talks on behalf of the American side, created massive local and international interest. Naturally, Jan Cushing invited the then-unmarried Kissinger to one of her now-famous Paris dinners, and naturally he accepted on a regular basis. It was only a matter of time before Jan, rather in the manner of Lady Hamilton, began a high-profile friendship with Henry Kissinger which was conducted in the press around the world. Freddie, by now having adopted the role of Sir William Hamilton, ignored all this, and would have happily continued to do so, but Jan was bored with him and also with Paris by now. There was peace in Vietnam, so Henry went home. It was a time to be single again – but keep the name Cushing – and move the salon to New York. Jan was not yet thirty, and there were many adventures ahead. Adventures that included brief affairs with Frank Sinatra, Warren Beatty, Gianni Agnelli, Bill Paley, and Stavros Niarchos. There remained a final parting gift for Freddie, who had not received an annual bonus that year from Lehman. Jan telephoned his boss (a man shortly to become Treasury Secretary) to inform him that unless her husband received a substantial bonus forthwith, Henry Kissinger would be induced to instruct the IRS to begin an investigation into the boss's personal tax affairs. Freddie duly received a generous Christmas bonus. And the die was cast for many such similar phone calls in the future.

A couple of years later, in a massive roll of the dice, I stumbled into this surreal world.

CHAPTER SEVEN

A Midsummer Night's Dream

'A S SOON AS YOU GET TO THE CHURCH INTRODUCE YOURSELF to Norman Mailer,' Jan instructed me on the morning of our wedding.

'You'll recognise him in the front row next to my parents. And my bridesmaids will be waiting there too. Introduce yourself to them. They are Jane Spencer-Churchill, Norris Mailer (wife of Norman Mailer), and Alexandra Schlesinger (married to historian Arthur). Pat (Kennedy) Lawford didn't make the flight.'

I nodded, by this time hoping that my dear mother wouldn't have been too disappointed in me and that my long-suffering father – who had organised the Greek Archbishop to officiate in the Greek Cathedral in London –wouldn't be too downhearted. My father put a brave face on it, but I knew he was deeply upset.

'It's not too late!' John Radziwiłł, my best man, urged me only half-laughing as he accompanied me that afternoon to church. And I knew he was right, but I didn't have the nerve to turn back now. The guests were waiting, the room at the Dorchester prepared, the newspaper announcements made. I swallowed hard and pressed on.

On arrival at St. Sophia Cathedral, I recognised Norman Mailer from his book cover photographs. I duly introduced myself to this short, stocky, middle-aged man with twinkling clear blue eyes and a bucketload of charisma.

'Wow!' Norman said, 'Manoli Olympitis ... Manoli Olympitis ... great name.'

These were the first words spoken to me by the extraordinary, brilliant character who would figure so largely in my life for the next thirty years. I shook hands with the bridesmaids and waited, standing silently between John and my brother Niki while my mind wandered back across the previous week.

I had asked Jan to convert to the Greek Orthodox Church and was not surprised when she agreed immediately. Anything to escape the religion into which she'd been born. I was however surprised by the reaction of the Greek Bishop from whom I sought assistance with considerable trepidation. After all, the Orthodox Church is not known for its pro-Jewish stance.

'This is absolutely no problem,' he stated gravely. 'We do not recognise this religion. It does not exist. I can perform the baptism whenever you both wish.'

I still think it is ironic that, had Jan been a Christian, but a Roman Catholic or Protestant, conversion to Greek Orthodox would have been a far more problematic procedure.

As it was, I acted as godfather at Jan's baptism, Billy and Virginia Salomon (of Salomon Brothers), stood in for Jan's parents.

'Now you are completely without sin. Far less sin than I,' the Bishop had pronounced. He beamed at Jan after the service in which, beatifically virginal in a thin, white, cotton robe, standing in a basin for a font, she had been doused from head to toe in holy water.

I could not help but wonder whether that divine innocence would be measured in minutes, or in seconds.

In any event, the wedding took place a week later and dinner at the Dorchester Hotel was eventful for me only in that Norman Mailer and I formed an immediate rapport – indeed, I really cannot remember very much else. In between the usual toasts and throughout dinner, we were deep in conversation. I was in the midst of a complicated banking transaction and could not be away from the office for long, so Jan and

I had planned a very short honeymoon of two nights at the Compleat Angler at Marlow in Buckinghamshire. Norman was principally in the United Kingdom to promote the forthcoming publication of his novel *The Executioner's Song* (for which he subsequently won his second Pulitzer Prize), but he had no commitments for a couple of days and wanted to show Norris around Oxford, which is not far from Marlow. As a result, the Mailers stayed at the Compleat Angler as well, and we all toured Oxford together. This gave rise to the frequent and accurate newspaper observations that Norman and Norris had come on our honeymoon with us.

It was enormously endearing to see how nervous Norman was on that Sunday morning. Kenneth Tynan's review of his book was due out in the *Sunday Times*. Norman knew how much this would set the tone for the novel's broader reception in England, and how unpredictable Tynan could be. He needn't have worried. The review was a glowing appreciation of his work.

It also amused me that, walking past a High Street bookshop, I dragged Norman inside and asked a young female assistant whether they had any books by Norman Mailer. Norman was convinced they would have none. He was wrong of course, to his obvious relief, although unsurprisingly, the young girl did not recognise the renowned author standing before her.

Jan's enthusiasm for life in London predictably did not survive more than a few months. She felt ignored here. Not nearly enough fuss was made of her. Whilst we had an active social life most evenings, she was not the celebrated hostess here that she was in New York. Nor did London embrace her celebrity to the same extent as New York. Jan missed the press attention, the ability to call in favours from powerful friends, and the power to intimidate rivals or perceived enemies. Compounding this, I worked until late, getting home just in time for dinner. I often had to make overnight business trips, and there were a limited number of friends or acquaintances who did not need to work and were available to meet her for lunch. Jan was not the type to visit galleries, museums, or attend afternoon matinees. Nor can I recall her ever finishing a book.

Jan, however, did have a remarkable facility to entertain politicians and writers without either having read their books or understanding the basic political issues. This always amazed me. She had a talent for discussing a subject or book for just long enough not to be found out, and then changing the subject or switching the conversation to another guest. She was also brilliant in flattering the huge egos that usually surrounded her – unless she perceived some form of minor slight or realised that her charm wasn't working. Then, she would turn upon the unfortunate person, abusing them loudly until they left the party. This ensured that everyone who enjoyed both her hospitality and the opportunity to mingle with their perceived equals in congenial surroundings, always generously reciprocated with compliments about her.

In any event, Jan was desperate to resume her old way of life – to feel important again. An understanding Bankers Trust posted me to New York to head up investment banking there. We relinquished our rented flat in Rutland Gate, she gave away a yellow Labrador puppy called Greco that I had given her, and we crossed the Atlantic to move into her flat on 79th Street without a backward look. My married life in New York had begun.

With the extent of Jan's underlying volatility not yet apparent to me, life in the evenings was an endless series of dinners and openings. Well documented by the press, Jan was frequent hostess to her core group, which included the Mailers.* The lively, always fascinating level of mainly political conversation and debate was hardly surprising. Gene McCarthy, dramatically overestimating my resources, once

* Frequent guests at these gatherings were also the Schlesingers, the Radziwiłłs, George Plimpton, Margaux Hemingway, Steve and Jean Kennedy Smith, Pat Kennedy Lawford, Gene McCarthy, and Sam Spiegel.

confided he was considering another run at the Presidency and asked for my financial support. The debate was amplified by additional regular attendees,* as well as any up-and-coming artist or writer who had caught Jan's attention.

Jan's favourite gambit in the latter instance was to buy sufficient copies of a new author's book to place one on every seat around the table. This naturally had the effect of not only drawing everyone's attention to it, but also making the book an early conversation topic. One such struggling writer was Winston Groom. A Vietnam veteran, Winston had received excellent reviews for two wonderful, but initially commercially unsuccessful novels called *As Summers Die* and *Better Times Than These*, and we became close friends. A few years later, after I had left New York for good, Winston returned to his hometown of Mobile, Alabama, to write a novel he called *Forrest Gump*. He has never struggled since.

Even more luxurious than our home life were our summer vacations, and during early August in the summers of 1981 and 1982, we chartered a 180-foot motor-yacht by the name of *Spalmatori* on which we invited friends.† We sailed from Piraeus through the Cyclades Islands for about two weeks, visiting Stavros Niarchos and his sons Philip and Spyros on their island of Spetsopoula, then seeing George and Lita Livanos on Coronis, and finally dropping by Bluey and Caroline Mavroleon at Porto Heli. We would occasionally put into the island of Spetses to see which friends were holidaying there. Rupert Galliers-Pratt and Nigel Cayzer had become business partners as well as friends, and though we later predictably fell out, we did all have uproarious times together in the most comfortable circumstances. Life began to imitate art. I often felt I was peering in through a cinema window observing with some fascination a glamorous Technicolor film in which I had a leading role. And speaking

* It was at these parties that I had become acquainted with Farrah Fawcett, as well as meeting Miloš Forman, Swifty Lazar, Ahmet Ertegun, Paddy Chayefsky, Kurt Vonnegut, and Ryan O'Neal, who were all regulars.
† Our group of both years – made up of Charles and Jane Spencer-Churchill, Rupert and Alibee Galliers-Pratt, Nigel Cayzer, and my old friend Cliff Klenk with his Austrian girlfriend – nicknamed the yacht the 'Spermatori'.

of life, films, and art, I was soon, along with Rupert and Nigel, to become embroiled in a film financing project in Los Angeles – more of that soon.

The South of France, or more accurately the Hotel du Cap in Antibes, was always Jan's and my destination for the last two weeks of August, so that we would be back in Newport in time for Labour Day weekend, and the annual dance at the Reading Room, the oldest gentleman's club in America. At that time, the Hotel du Cap retained much of the glamorous type of international clientele for which it had become renowned since the 1930s.* Hollywood was always well represented: Sam Spiegel cruising by from St. Tropez on his yacht; Gregory Peck and Roger Moore often arriving from Saint-Paul-de-Vence with their wives; Johnny Carson usually taking the cabana on the sea next to ours, with different wives all seemingly named Joanne or Joanna; and many other well-known show-biz folk who happened to be in the area would make a point of calling in to see what was happening and to be seen. Gregoir, the swimming instructor at the pool who gave our son his first lesson, was a living link with a previous, legendary era: He had taught the young Prince Aly Khan to swim. The latter, more recently, had spent his honeymoon with Rita Hayworth at the hotel.

For our two weeks, we reserved the private villa in the grounds. Once a simple wooden structure, it had been converted into a luxurious, marble, four-bedroom villa, located between the Eden Roc beachside restaurant and the main hotel, but discreetly hidden by immaculate pines and cypress trees. A great advantage was the ability to have timely room service from the restaurant. And for the second weekend of our stay we would give a large dinner on the villa's terrace, with music provided by the Eden Roc.

A few days before that second weekend of August 1982, Jan was in a state of high excitement. She had spotted Barbra Streisand with her then-boyfriend Jon Peters checking in. Although she knew neither of

---

* English business tycoons, such as James Hanson, Gordon White, Max Rayne, were regular guests. Freddy Heineken, who had a house nearby, was always dropping in, as were Gianni Agnelli, Henry Ford, Al Taubman, Gunter Sachs, the Flick brothers, and assorted members of the Greek shipping fraternity.

them, Jan was determined that Streisand would come to dinner. But how to achieve this? She decided that Jon Peters would provide the answer. She watched and she waited.

That afternoon, Jon Peters – a highly successful Beverley Hills hairdresser-turned-film-producer – was sunbathing on a diving raft anchored offshore when Jan surfaced nearby and climbed aboard to take a short break in the sun. She turned to smile at him. Peters, pleasant and easy going as he was, could have hardly failed to have been impressed by the beautiful, tanned blonde in the white swimsuit that engaged him in amusing conversation and was clearly a fellow American. It was not long before a friendly relationship had been established. Jan casually mentioned she had the private villa, where she was hosting an annual dinner there with her husband that weekend. She dropped into the conversation that the guests would include a former Prime Minister of France, as well as a former Prime Minister of Great Britain who was coming with Sam Spiegel. Jon Peters was extremely impressed, subsequently passing this on to Barbra Streisand, as Jan knew he would. She was careful not to go any further.

The following day, by amazing coincidence, Jan bumped into Jon Peters again. By now they were Americans abroad together, practically old pals. At this point, Jan offered an invitation to the two of them for dinner. Jon Peters readily accepted for himself, but thought that, although Streisand might well come, he could not guarantee it. He did mention that this was their first time in the South of France, they had both expected the dress code in the evening to be considerably more formal, and that Streisand had brought several outfits she was dying to wear. Jan instantly observed that her dinner was formal for the women and smart casual for the men. She would be delighted if Peters came, she added cleverly, alone or otherwise. She would have an invitation delivered to their room confirming the time and dress of the dinner.

This was Jan at her best. She was perfectly capable of exaggerating her guest lists when it suited her, but this time she had not. Her friend Florence Grinda was bringing former premier Raymond Barre, and

Sam Spiegel was bringing his house guest Sir Edward Heath. The others were all attractive international personalities, including Mick Flick and Barbara Allen.

Right up to the last minute, we did not know whether Barbra Streisand was coming. Sigrid, our son's German nanny, suddenly started to point excitedly in the direction of the main hotel; there, slowly walking towards us, her head elegantly wrapped in a green silk turban and accompanied by Jon Peters, Streisand came. She was charming that night. She had that wonderful combination of vulnerability and poise that is common to many artists of great talent. The vulnerability was increased by a nervousness, natural since she had never met either host, let alone any of the guests – although she and Sam later found much to chat about. I gently took her in hand over drinks to help her relax, then steered her into dinner beside me as she gradually began to unwind and feel comfortable. I have always thought it was brave of her to come to dinner with a group of strangers, especially given her great celebrity status, but she enjoyed herself immensely, everyone was kind and not overly friendly, and Jon Peters continually looked after her.

I met Ted Heath for the first time that evening too. A good natured and extremely cultured man beneath the gruff exterior, he would turn out to be a great friend to me in later life.

Another friendship I struck up that night was with Cecil Everley, a well-known café-society figure on both sides of the Atlantic. As a young, handsome but effete footman employed by the Earl of Beauchamp at Madresfield Court (a family that had inspired Evelyn Waugh to write his novel *Brideshead Revisited*), Cecil had been swept up by the wealthy Count Pecci-Blunt who installed him as a male mistress in a small house in the South of France. Introduced to the great social hostesses of the day, Cecil had become a popular single man at their dinners ever since. His success as a talented painter of seascapes (I have two of them) added to his allure. Pecci-Blunt had bequeathed Cecil his entire fortune and his homes in Cap-d'Ail, California, and New York. Now a most elegant, wealthy figure in his early seventies, Cecil was a favourite 'walker' to many powerful women of a certain age. He was particularly close to Princess Grace of Monaco, a regular guest at La Rondine whenever Prince Rainier was otherwise occupied, and it was there at Cecil's house I met several times the former Grace Kelly. I found her very approachable from the beginning, interested in everyone, great fun, and always happy to dance with people she liked. We got on extremely well and danced together a good deal. I was immensely saddened when she died in that awful car accident three years later.

CHAPTER EIGHT

The End of the Beginning

P ROFESSIONALLY SPEAKING, NEW YORK BEGAN ON A HIGH NOTE
for me. I was working hard to put together a significant loan for the
East German central bank – Deutsche Aussenhandelsbank – on highly
competitive terms. The other US banks decided to publicly boycott the
transaction on the ostensible grounds that lending to East Germany, or
any other of the Soviet satellites, would free up funds which would allow
the Soviet Union to spend more on nuclear arms. The real reason was
they wanted more profitable terms. The chairman of Morgan Guaranty
telephoned my chairman calling for me to be fired, and within that rar-
efied banking world a full-scale row took place.

Jan knew the Sulzberger family who owned the *New York Times* and
obtained an introduction for me to the executive editor. I submitted an
opinion piece entitled 'Keep up the Loans to Eastern Europe'. This was
published on a Sunday morning in February 1980, in the midst of the fund
raising, and was of assistance in persuading most of the major European
banks, and all four of the leading UK ones, to make the transaction a great
success, even without US participation. My argument had been that only
by encouraging the seeds of prosperity in Eastern European countries
would the West be able, over time, to dismantle communism, bringing
them into the capitalist fold. This was not new, but events bore this out
nine years later of course, with the fall of the Berlin Wall. Much more
than this however, I have treasured the complimentary letter written to

me at the time by Arthur Schlesinger, not only the most distinguished American modern historian of his generation, but also a national security adviser to President Kennedy during the Cuban Missile Crisis. And I never cashed the 100-dollar cheque from the *New York Times*. I framed it to hang proudly in the guest lavatory.

Creature comforts away from the office went far beyond extremely comfortable. At home, staff were running like hot and cold water, cars with drivers were always outside. Jan's favourite restaurants were La Grenouille, 21 Club, Elaine's, Nicola's, Mortimer's, and Le Bilboquet, at all of which the best table was waiting. Travel was always by Concorde across the Atlantic, first class everywhere else, and by private plane for trips within a couple of hours from New York.

Holiday destinations during the winter were rented houses in the Bahamas and Jamaica, or Palm Beach's most central social spot: the Bath and Tennis Club. Many of the families of American commerce and industry lived nearby,* their perpetual sunshine further brightened by a steady consumption of cocktails. Here, they rubbed shoulders with well-known celebrities from the entertainment industry – Cliff Robertson and Dina Merrill among others – together with those affluent Cuban families, such as Bacardi and Fanjul, their wealth safely stored in America beyond the reach of Fidel Castro.

This colourful kaleidoscope of elegantly dressed, attractive people, against the backdrop of the old-fashioned, plantation style, tropical green and cream furnishings of the 'B&T' created a vista reminiscent of more glamorous, bygone eras. So I pulled up in surprise when confronted by the incongruous sight of an old lady, dressed in rags, sitting alone at a table in the dining area, staring out to sea, an empty coffee cup at her elbow. I asked an established member who she was.

'Lili Damita,' came the sad reply. 'You remember her? The star from the thirties who married Errol Flynn when he was unknown?'

I nodded dumbly, recalling the image of a stunning, vivacious brunette.

* Including Honeywell, IBM, Corning (Glass) Inc., R. J. Reynolds Tobacco Company, and Citibank.

'She had a son with Errol – Sean Flynn. He was a war photographer. Disappeared in Vietnam years ago, now presumed dead. But she hasn't given up. She's certain he's still alive. The last address Sean had for her was the Club, and she's convinced he's coming back here. She's lost her mind with grief. She sits and waits for him at that table every day. People say they had their last lunch right there.'

A rather more amusing incident took place at the tiny airport at Martha's Vineyard. We had chartered a plane to visit our friend Peter Sharpe – owner of the Carlyle Hotel – for Memorial Weekend. As is often the case on the Vineyard, fog had suddenly descended on Sunday evening, delaying all flights. The airport runway was lined with private planes waiting for the weather to lift and for clearance to take off. Our pilot was apologetically escorting us into the hut which passed for a terminal building, when Jan spotted Jackie Kennedy with her children, Caroline and John Jr., perched at the coffee bar, waiting also. Quick as a flash, Jan turned to the pilot.

'A thousand bucks if you get us off before Jackie,' she said quietly. The startled pilot nodded imperceptibly as he left, while we went to greet Jackie.

'Hi there. Just arrived?' Jackie's light voice was as breathless as ever, 'Isn't this a bore. Oh well, hopefully it won't be too long.'

'Hopefully,' said Jan.

We chatted for about half an hour, Jackie introducing me to her children. The fog was beginning to recede. The loudspeaker system came to life, and Jan's name was announced. Our flight was cleared, and we should board. Jackie could not cover her surprise, but if she was annoyed she certainly did not show it. Wishing each other a safe journey, we said goodbye. I have rarely seen Jan as pleased and self-satisfied as she was throughout the trip back home. The pilot was happy too.

Rather less happy and far less satisfying was the experience of finding a summer resort house close to New York to buy, so that I would be able to continue working in June and July. This was my first realisation of how many enemies Jan had made among the older, conservative families who still controlled the membership of those beach clubs around which the social life of the most desirable resorts centred. We spent our first summer in Southampton, renting a beautifully converted barn from Ahmet Ertegun, my Rolling Stones host of nearly a decade earlier. Jan entertained there with great style and gusto, but this did not help our application to the Southampton Beach Club the following year. Fishers Island became the next destination. The same entertainment formula failed again, despite many indications that we would be welcomed as members.

Stung, on the third summer we turned to Newport, Rhode Island, where the Spouting Rock Beach Club (Bailey's Beach) was the grandest of them all – founded by the Astors and the Vanderbilts in the late 1800s. The direct predecessor of the Bath and Tennis Club in Palm Beach, this was particularly dangerous territory since the Cushing family held great sway, and of course Jan had been married to Freddie Cushing. Fortunately, I was able to genuinely befriend Freddie and his elder brother Howard, a senior governor of the club. Jan behaved herself for once. We squeaked in. Soon afterwards, with the help of a large mortgage, I bought a charming five-bedroom house with staff quarters and a two-bedroom guest annex close to the centre of town. Called Clover Patch, it was just down the avenue from Clarendon Court, famously the setting of the musical *High Society*, and infamously the scene of the alleged murder attempt on the heiress and socialite Sunny von Bülow by her husband Claus.* In the summer of '82, this morbid situation attracted a close friend of Jan's, who, as far as I was concerned at least, was rather an unwelcome visitor.

The sensational trial in Newport of Claus von Bülow for the attempted murder of his wife, Sunny, was due to take place. She was

---

* Nearby, on Thames Street, was St. Mary's Roman Catholic Church in which John and Jackie Kennedy had married, and Hammersmith Farm, the estate owned by Jackie's mother and stepfather – where the young couple had spent the first part of their honeymoon – was on the edge of town.

still in a coma from an injected overdose of insulin. As mentioned, the scene of the alleged crime was Clarendon Court, at the time of the trial still the home of Alexander and Ala Auersperg, Sunny's children by her first husband Prince Alfie von Auersperg. It was a weird coincidence that Alfie himself was also in a coma from which he too never regained consciousness. I knew Alex and Ala well through Jan. I often had dinner with them and occasionally played tennis with Alexander. They were both active members of the Beach, dropping in frequently for lunch.

The trial split the Beach membership down the middle. Most of the younger group believed that Claus was guilty. He seemed a sinister personality to them, and Alex and Ala were their friends. Of the older members, the men for the most part also believed in Claus' guilt, while the older ladies, who actually wielded great power at the Beach, defended him fiercely. They had all been charmed over the years by Claus. For a while, until Claus' conviction (later overturned on appeal), arguments raged around the Club, friendships formed over many years were stretched to breaking point. Personally, I was scrupulously neutral, although Jan was ardently against Claus. I had never known Sunny. Whenever I had seen her at the Beach, she had appeared a distant, solitary figure. Still beautiful, but with an aura of great sadness. Claus, on the other hand, was a jovial, cultured man-about-town who made a great effort with everyone. I always liked him, but he could sometimes come across as a little disdainful – he cultivated a certain diffidence. Nevertheless, he moved to London with his daughter Cosima after it was all over and had no trouble reconnecting with his old English circle, nor taking up the threads of his old life over here. He died, much missed, in May 2019, his subsequent memorial service packed to the rafters.

While the trial was at its peak, Jan's close friend, the writer Truman Capote, came to stay. Truman had of course written the bestselling book *In Cold Blood*. He and Norman Mailer had pioneered 'faction', which was reportage in the form of a novel, and he had taken a morbid interest in the von Bülow case.

I have to say that I never understood how Truman could have been so lionised by his 'swans', many of the most powerful, well-known, and glamorous women in America. Physically tiny, his voice was a high-pitched, nasal whine. His face, whilst striking when a young man, resembled by now a malevolent lizard. Truman was certainly a wonderful, rightly celebrated writer, with a quick acerbic wit. But he was a fundamentally cruel, deeply flawed individual, constantly betraying friendships and confidences whilst frequently drunk or under the influence of drugs. Great talent aside, the resemblance of his nature to Jan's was remarkable. No wonder they were so close. And in the end, although a natural 'walker' of women, an amusing extra man at a dinner party, a brilliantly gifted writer, his vindictive qualities betrayed him. Having publicly announced he was writing a series of short stories which would expose indirectly their private lives, Truman was directly shunned, then socially blacklisted by his precious 'swans'. He died alone of a drug overdose at the age of sixty.

To me, Truman was always extremely rude, in a pathetic, childish way. He had a habit of first ignoring me for some time, then asking me a question in his high, falsetto voice, then pointedly looking at the ceiling, whilst loudly chanting 'na, na, na, naaa, na' to drown out my answer.

I found this extraordinary and asked Norman Mailer what it was all about. Norman had known Truman well since they had both burst simultaneously upon the New York literary scene in their early twenties. Although polar opposites, they respected and understood each other. This is how Norman described the young Capote to me. They were both newly famous and had arranged to meet in Norman's local bar in Brooklyn before going on together to some literary event nearby. The tables were crowded with tough-looking, drunken truck drivers and manual workers. Norman was propping up the bar with a drink, waiting. The door suddenly opened to reveal a diminutive, black velvet-suited Truman Capote, a matching black opera cloak fastened around his neck. He instantly became the focal point of scornful stares. Obscene comments were shouted at him. 'Oh God,' muttered Norman, bracing himself, 'this is going to get ugly'. Truman was standing next to Norman at the bar. He slowly turned around and faced the crowd, staring them down. He said nothing, but such was the aura of vicious evil emanating from his tiny frame, that the crowd fell silent. Cowed, they averted their gaze. 'I've never seen anything like it,' Norman said. 'It was incredible. They were terrified of him. You don't fuck with Truman'.

'But as far as Jan is concerned, you have to understand,' Norman explained, 'that Truman has been in love with Jan for years, despite being gay. I am sure he always secretly believed he would marry Jan someday. He hates you for getting in the way.'

My own career was now taking a completely new direction. Together with Richard Berman, a good friend from Bankers Trust who headed up the mergers and acquisitions division, I left the bank and we started our own tiny boutique investment company. Naturally, this did not present the risk it would normally have been for me in light of Jan's income and assets, but business was progressing reasonably well. That is, until I had the dubious pleasure of meeting Ron Perelman, an aggressive dealmaker, married to Jan's cousin, Faith Golding.

As you may remember, Faith and Jan were the joint beneficiaries of the Golding Trusts. Perelman was at the beginning of his career. Not yet the owner of Revlon, Technicolor, or Marvel Entertainment Group – not yet highly successful and one of the richest men of New York. But he had managed to make himself a trustee for his wife, and Jan's lawyers were concerned that he might access the joint trust funds for the benefit of his own business (although there was no evidence of this). They therefore proposed an equitable division of the trusts so that each beneficiary would have their own assets. This was agreed. I was asked to negotiate such a distribution with Perelman. This proved an unpleasant experience, since I thought Perelman an unpleasant man.

A person of small stature, he had a towering ego together with obvious anger-management issues. Even his own lawyers were terrified of him; he would rant and rave, and it seemed to me that the only negotiating approach Perelman understood was one of maximum confrontation. His strategy was to ask for the moon on every issue, refuse to compromise, and begin shouting maniacally at all and sundry until he obtained a measure of agreement. Whilst this crude approach is not uncommon on Wall Street, where social skills are in short supply, and indeed it seems to have stood Perelman well for the future, it was never going to be effective with me.

This was getting us nowhere, and so without warning Perelman went for what he perceived was the jugular. He correctly surmised that Jan and I were, to a large extent, dependent on the income which the trust dividends provided her, and he managed to temporarily halt these payments. Jan's lifestyle was far more expensive than Faith's, and having just replaced my Bankers Trust salary with start-up costs for the new business, I was in no position to take up the slack. With a gun held at our heads, we started to race through capital outside the trusts at an alarming rate. We tried to reinstate the dividends by resorting to legal action through the Surrogate's Court, which piled up considerable further expense, and delay upon delay. Somewhat desperate, I began to arrange borrowings against future assets, but could not understand Jan's remarkably calm demeanour and apparent lack of any anxiety over the financial straits into which we were hurtling. And Christmas was just around the corner.

'For Heaven's sake, stop worrying. I'll call Sidney Korshak,' she said.

'Who?' I was perplexed.

'Sidney will fix it.'

'Who the hell is Sidney?'

'Sidney, Sidney Korshak,' Jan replied patiently, 'he'll fix it.'

'What on earth are you talking about?'

'Didn't you read that *New York Times* article last year?' Jan was looking smug, '"A Word from Sidney is a Word from the Boys"? He's the most powerful man in organised crime. And he's my friend. A good friend. But you'll have to go and see him. I'll call him now.'

An assistant told her that Mr. Korshak would her call back. He did, about an hour later. They talked for a while and Jan came into my study.

'Sidney will see you on Friday. The Four Seasons Hotel in Chicago, the penthouse apartment, straight after lunch for two o'clock. Don't worry. Just explain everything to him. It will all work out.'

I was incredulous. 'Jan, this is not a movie. This is not fantasy time. Are you sure you know what you're talking about?'

Jan quietly explained to me the facts of life in the context of Sidney Korshak's background. There was practically nothing he couldn't fix, if he wanted to.

Pushing away serious doubts, but with several misgivings, I prepared for the trip. Landing at O'Hare Airport on schedule two days later, I took a taxi to the Four Seasons Hotel, and asked reception to call the penthouse, giving my name. I was ushered into an express elevator and it shot me up to the forty-sixth floor. The suite was a large apartment covering the entire floor, with a small office just inside the front door that was occupied by a pretty secretary and two stocky male assistants. The housekeeper who had opened the door waved me past this and down a short corridor into a typically bland, but comfortable hotel sitting room. A powerfully built, bear-like man in his early sixties rose from an armchair to greet me.

'Hi, I'm Sidney Korshak.' A large paw stretched out towards me and we shook hands as sharp, blue eyes from beneath a mane of greying brown hair appraised me. He gestured to the sofa.

'How do you do,' I sat down. 'Thank you for seeing me.'

He nodded, 'No problem. How's Jan? Her parents?'

The voice was gruff but friendly and, as we exchanged the usual courtesies, I found myself warming to Sidney's avuncular charm. The phone beside him rang suddenly; he answered. A short, lively conversation with someone called Bob ensued. The film producer Robert Evans, as the caller turned out to be, was obviously raising finance, and after promising Evans both his support and his affection, Sidney turned slowly back to me.

'Now, kid. What's the problem?'

I explained the fruitless negotiation, the freezing of the dividends, the lawsuit, my new business, our need to unblock funds.

'Sure,' he nodded, 'okay, I'll fix it. No problem.'

I thought he hadn't understood. I started to try to outline some of the difficult legal issues – after all, he was a lawyer – but he interrupted me brusquely.

'Kid, I said it's no problem!' The change of tone was sudden. Intimidating. Then the friendly, smiling uncle quickly returned. 'It's Christmas, Sunday. Go back home to your family where you belong. Give Jan my love. Have a great time, don't worry about anything.'

My time was over. After a few pleasantries, I took my leave in a disbelieving daze. I do not remember the trip back to New York.

'How did it go?' Jan asked.

'I don't know. I don't think he understood the issues. He didn't give me a chance to explain,' I replied haltingly.

'Did he say it would be all right or not?' Jan said impatiently.

'Yes. I think so.'

'Then it will be. Now forget about it.' That particular conversation ended.

I still couldn't take any of this seriously but managed to put it out of my mind for the time being. The holidays passed, and about a week later, my lawyers called to tell me that the judge had called an urgent all-parties meeting in the Surrogate's District Court in three days' time. I was amazed. It had all been going so slowly. Everyone had seemed to be dragging their feet. Jan just laughed at me.

At the hearing, a highly focused, elderly female judge announced that she wanted both sides to reach a settlement within ten days or incur the wrath of the court. She enumerated the legal issues involved, as she saw them, and then reinstated the dividend payments with immediate effect. I stared, still disbelieving, across at a strangely silent Perelman next to his wife and their impassive lawyers. Everyone agreed to divide the trust assets equitably in the days to come. It had taken me a while, but I finally realised the unlimited power of great influence in America and the varying ways in which justice can be achieved there.

CHAPTER NINE

The Beginning of the End

T HE 28TH OF FEBRUARY 1981 WAS ONE OF THE VERY BEST DAYS of my life. My son John was born and named after my ecstatic father who rushed across the Atlantic to visit his first grandchild. The date had been chosen by Jan some time before, because it fitted well with her crowded social schedule, and an 'emergency' caesarean section had been arranged at an expensive hospital in New York well in advance. A caesarean birth could only legally take place in the city if the infant's life was in danger and thus in an emergency. For an appropriate financial consideration, and as a result of remarkable psychic powers, such emergencies were frequently foreseen. I too, however, was overjoyed. A cosy nursery had been created in the 79th Street apartment with Enid Blyton characters such as Noddy and Big Ears painted on the walls. A 'Norland nanny' had been hired to take charge. John's childhood began whilst life for us resumed its previous course. More or less.

Sadly, Jan's insecurities were becoming increasingly obvious even to my naïve younger self. When I had been at Bankers Trust, she had often called work colleagues when she couldn't reach me to check whether I really was in the meeting I had told her about. Although merely embarrassing at first, this kind of now extreme, erratic behaviour, her illogical disbelief of my movements during a normal working day, her bombardment of me with calls several times an hour, was paranoid. She started to have me watched and followed by private detectives whenever I (or she) was out of town. I had given her no reason to mistrust me, but her answer was that she freely admitted to not trusting any man. Norman Mailer liked to describe this as 'Jan's passion for verification', but I was suffocating. I insisted she needed help; indeed, she had visited her psychoanalyst three times a week for many years, but he just told her what she wanted to hear and took the money.

Jan's now axiomatic hostility to anyone close to me who was not also a friend of hers was becoming intolerable too. She detested my friendship with Raymond simply because we were inseparable friends; even my younger brother, Niki, to whom I had always been very close, she resented. Any girl I spoke to for more than a minute whom Jan did not know, she would turn on, usually threatening violence. And of course, if any friend happened to be female, Jan could go to insane lengths to intimidate them and alienate them from me.

A classic example of this was the instance of Diana Trafford's visit to New York. Diana was very much part of my group in London, a most attractive, properly nice girl, and a very good friend. She telephoned me at the office to tell me she was in town for about a week, camping on a girlfriend's sofa. I told her that was ridiculous, that she must stay with us; she should call Jan at home to let her know when a good time would be to arrive. I gave her the phone number, and then called Jan to prepare her. Jan was delighted. 'No problem,' she would organise it all, she said.

When I got home that evening, I expected to find Diana happily ensconced in a guest room, preparing for drinks before dinner. There was no sign of her. Jan shook her head. No, she had heard nothing from Diana; no, Diana hadn't called, she certainly hadn't turned up. Puzzled, I telephoned the girlfriend she had originally planned to stay with, but there was no reply. I reluctantly accepted Jan's observation that Diana had obviously changed her plans and had arranged to stay somewhere else. But it was completely out of character for Diana not to have let me know, even if Jan was correct in her waspish assumption that Diana had probably met someone and carelessly not bothered to follow up with us. 'Some friend of yours she must be,' Jan said nastily, 'I hear she's a slut anyway. Probably holed up with a man at some hotel.' I ignored this last remark, telephoned again a couple of times over the next few days, but to no avail. What more could I do. I forgot about it.

The epilogue of this story is that about three years later, sometime after my divorce from Jan, I was at the bar at Annabel's with two business partners when Diana happened to come in together with a charming young Viscount to whom she had just got engaged. I greeted her warmly, only to be met with a decidedly frosty reception. Bewildered, I asked her what was wrong and why she hadn't turned up that night in New York.

'Because of your bloody wife,' she answered curtly. 'Thanks a bunch!'

'What?' I was confused, but an awful truth was dawning.

'You really don't know?' came the still-angry, disbelieving response. I admitted total ignorance.

'When I telephoned her as you told me to, your wife said I had two choices. Either I could take a cab to Kennedy Airport where there would be a first-class ticket waiting for me on the last flight to London, or I could return the next day, in economy class, in a wheelchair, my broken legs in plaster.' Diana was still furious.

'Well, I'd heard about your wife, so I flew back that night. Thanks for nothing.'

I don't think Diana has ever believed I had known absolutely nothing. I can't blame her. She hasn't spoken to me since.

When I remarked to my partners standing next to me that this was an incredible turn of events, they looked at me pityingly.

'But everyone in London knows that story,' they said.

The days when I could shrug off Jan's mercurial moods, ignore the fevered imagination that led to unwarranted attacks on erstwhile friends, and dismiss all the lies designed to provoke me into revealing imaginary indiscretions were passing. It seemed I could do nothing to change it. With the active support of her psychoanalyst, she was in complete denial. In addition, I had a son who needed to be brought up with some semblance of normality.

My first step was to use new business opportunities to create some physical distance from Jan for at least part of the time. The film financing business was an excellent start.

I had been introduced to Rupert Galliers-Pratt and his brother Nigel by a mutual friend, Charles Spencer-Churchill, the younger brother of the Duke of Marlborough. Initially, Rupert was seeking to expand his modest UK-based real-estate business with one or two opportunities in the US. Nigel had been working with a British merchant bank from which he had recently resigned. There, he had been developing the concept of a new completion-guarantee company for the film industry, but his bank had ultimately decided against it. Nigel was determined to create such a company on his own. He had approached Rupert for funding, who in turn approached me. We both thought the idea had merit and agreed to put up between the two of us the 200,000 dollars that Nigel needed to put his plan into action. The brothers came from wealthy establishment families on both their parents' sides, but as the eldest, only Rupert had access to their funds for the time being.

To explain my new investment for a moment: It was then, and I believe still is, the case that if an independent producer wishes to borrow from a bank to make a film, the bank will require a guarantee from a well-resourced third party. This third party will guarantee that if the production runs out of funds before completion of the film, then it will provide sufficient finance to finish it and allow a general release. In return, the third party receives a guarantee fee of six per cent of the film's original budget up front.

This does sound fraught with risk but was not for two reasons: First, Nigel had made an arrangement with the Hayward insurance syndicate at Lloyd's of London to lay off virtually all our risk for three per cent of the budget, thus theoretically leaving us with a three per cent cut for no risk at all. Given an average historic budget for a feature film of fifty million dollars, this meant 1.5 million dollars to us per picture. The second reason was that it was accepted that the guarantor would have their own accountants on the set every day, countersigning all cheques, together with the power to take over production the moment that it exceeded the agreed budget. This last fact alone usually ensured that the director stayed within budget. The knowledge that their creation would be butchered just to get it into the can was too awful for any self-respecting director to contemplate. The flaw of course was that in the event of more than a couple of insurance claims, our premiums would soon be raised to a point where the company was no longer profitable. But that would hopefully be avoided for a lengthy period of time while we built the company's reserves. We called it Global Guarantees.

As far as competition was concerned, the preeminent player was Richard Soames' Film Finances which had originally been financed by the Bank of America, but the market was desperate for an additional alternative. American Express had dipped their toe in the water through a one-girl office, but was not giving her sufficient support to make a difference. There was no one else. This was the opportunity Nigel had found.

Now we had to form not only a serious board of directors, but one that could command sufficient respect in Hollywood to obtain new business. There was my record as an international banker, and I brought in my friend Angus Lightfoot Walker, the retired founding chairman of the large US conglomerate the City Investing Company of New York. Gus was well known in Los Angeles, where he had successfully done business since the war. He then brought in our star turn, Carl Foreman, to act as chairman. For the benefit of younger readers, Carl Foreman was a legendary writer/director/producer. His first major success had been the screenplay of *High Noon*, for which he received an Oscar. Other notable successes were the screenplay of *The Bridge on the River Kwai*, written while he was blacklisted during the McCarthy witch-hunt era, and the enormous hit *The Guns of Navarone*, which Carl had produced and for which he had won the Best Film Oscar. That he agreed to join us was a major coup. For me, it was a particular pleasure since we became close colleagues. One aspect of this was to provide another major turning point in my life, as you will discover. Rupert naturally joined us on the board, Nigel was chief executive.

To reminisce for a moment about Carl Foreman, here is a small digression. He had showed me one morning the latest draft of his new screenplay entitled 'The Yellow Jersey'. This was to be an adventure film set within that famous cycling race, the Tour de France. Carl was agonising over an appropriate ending. I was flattered to be asked and had offered an opinion which was peremptorily dismissed, but I was already much impressed with the storyline.

Without really thinking, I said, 'Carl, write me in, please.'

'What?'

'Carl,' I repeated impatiently, 'write me in.'

'Into what?' he asked, not unreasonably.

'Into the script,' my tone turning terse.

'You want to be in the movie?' Carl began to laugh, 'You want to become an actor?'

'Carl, I want to be a star!' I replied, annoyed that he should think this so amusing.

'But Manoli,' Carl's voice became soothing and slightly condescending, 'don't you understand why people become actors and why actors want to become stars?'

'I don't. And I don't really care,' I rushed heedlessly on, 'please just write me in!'

'Well, let me explain.' Carl was at his most avuncular now. 'Actors want to be you. Stars want to be you. Don't you understand? They all want to dress like you, look like you, have had your education, have your lifestyle, have been to the places you've been, do everything you do. But they can only act like you. They can't be you. You are the real thing. The real McCoy. Why would you want to be like them? Archie Leach wanted to be Cary Grant. Cary Grant tried to be like you, but you are the real thing,' he was emphatic, 'so stop it. It's a silly idea!'

'My goodness, Carl,' I said thoughtfully, suddenly feeling very silly and rather important at the same time, 'I do believe you're right.

What a ridiculous thought that was. Yes, after all, I am the real thing. I am me!'

'Exactly,' replied Carl briskly. 'Now let's get some lunch.'

It was not until that night, whilst rerunning the conversation in my mind with a considerable sense of self-importance, that I realised what had happened. I had been rejected by a master of rejection. A man who, throughout a distinguished film career, had turned down hundreds of actors for hundreds of roles, but had still made them feel good about themselves. Precisely as he had achieved with me. It was probably his standard rejection speech, but it was brilliant psychology.

In any event, the company was successful from the start, largely owing to Carl's introductions and Nigel's good work, accomplished with only one assistant and one secretary. Whilst we rented a small back office around the corner from the Beverly Hills Hotel, our 'front of house' de facto became Bungalow 10 of the hotel in which both Rupert and I stayed when we were visiting. Nigel had moved to Los Angeles and taken an apartment in the Hollywood hills.

And this was the point. Our activities had rapidly reached the stage where I could justify spending one week every month in Los Angeles. The price I knew was that Jan would have me followed and watched around the clock.

In London also, a new opportunity had presented itself, again through a connection of Rupert's. Greville Howard (now a Conservative peer) had identified a small listed pawnbroker called Harvey & Thompson as an interesting public vehicle for us to control and expand. We formed a syndicate of family and friends to buy a controlling interest, Rupert became chairman. This justified another week every month in London. With one eye on the future, I bought a small flat in Eaton Place. It was to be decorated by a former girlfriend and interior designer, Sofia Stainton.

Life with Jan was considerably easier to handle on the basis of two weeks out of four in New York. I could just about put up with the hysterical phone calls if they were at a distance of over 1,000 miles. The embarrassing public incidents in New York were halved. I could continue to spend quality time with my son John, both in the City and in Newport.

I was, indeed still am, fond of Newport. I had made great friends from among the members of Bailey's Beach Club. The club itself is a relaxed, but busy hub of activities. An old-fashioned drinks bar with delicious cocktails was next to the informal dining area, served by a sea food/salad bar and a hamburger bar. The swimming pool was further down the beach, cabanas lined both the pool and the seashore. The tennis courts were behind. For children of all ages, a supervised 'sports group' arranged various activities both indoors and outside from the morning until lunch, thus providing parents with a respite and the children with a superior social circle which would endure for the rest of their lives.

The town itself, with its cheerful, inexpensive cafes, bars, and restaurants attracted students and young people throughout the summer months. The harbour has a strong sailing tradition that dates from colonial times and thus became the base of the New York Yacht Club, the spiritual home of the America's Cup. The Yacht Club had been the title-holder since the first race against England in 1851, and Newport was the venue of every defence of the Cup, at four-year intervals since then. So, it was to Clover Patch, our house there, that my new friend Edward Heath, a keen sailor himself, came to stay for the 1983 defence of the Cup.

Ted stayed in our guest cottage with his Special Branch protection officers for a week. This flew past in a haze of dinner parties, yacht races, and interviews by the BBC, who were becoming excited with the strong showing of the British entry under Peter de Savary. It all culminated in a memorable ball – with music provided by Peter Duchin's band – which Jan and I threw for Ted and was attended by friends from the City, the Hamptons, and most of the Beach members, but alas did not prevent the British team from being eliminated by Alan Bond's Australia. Amid huge controversy surrounding its underwater extending keel, Australia finally beat the United States to take the Cup away from Newport. It has not returned since.

Ted was not the only famous Brit who came to Newport to support Peter de Savary and the British boat in the America's Cup, and it was also this year that I once again saw a close friend from the past.

Jan and I were invited to dinner one night by Senator and Mrs. Claiborne Pell. The dinner was in honour of their house guests, Prince and Princess Michael of Kent.

The latter I had known in the early 1970s when her name was Marie Christine Troubridge, and she had not yet met Prince Michael. Marie Christine was a successful interior designer who in fact decorated my flat in Brompton Square. We had developed a close friendship which had cooled before her engagement to Prince Michael. However, at that time, the two of us met to have a glass of champagne and toast her future. She had raised a glass to my future also and wished me luck, particularly, she said, 'because I don't expect we shall see each other socially again'. And given that she was about to join the royal family, who was I to disagree? Even if it did seem rather a high-handed statement at the time.

On this occasion in Newport, not wishing to appear over familiar or cause any embarrassment, I resolved that evening to act as if we had never met, unless or until Marie Christine wished it otherwise. But I had not foreseen her loyalty to an old friend.

While waiting with the other guests for the royal couple to come down for dinner, I checked the seating plan and unsurprisingly found my name on table six, the most junior table. Jan, I noted, was on table three.

The guests of honour swept in, Claiborne Pell began the introductions, and I patiently waited my turn.

'Your Royal Highnesses, may I present Mr. and Mrs. Manoli Olympitis.'

I bowed to Prince Michael, 'Sir.' He nodded back pleasantly.

I turned and bowed to Princess Michael. Jan went into full curtsy mode.

'Manoli!' Marie Christine exclaimed. 'How extraordinary! Claiborne, this is a dear friend from England. Where is he seated?'

Claiborne, momentarily confused, consulted the seating plan.

'Do please put him next to me,' she went on, 'I want to catch up.'

The senior Senator from Rhode Island had little choice. I was promoted to table one. Marie Christine and I had a lively conversation all throughout dinner, both to the chagrin of my wife, glaring over occasionally from the now relative wilderness of table three, and to the sudden admiration of all the other dinner guests who were now regarding me in a much more favourable light.

'Which one is your wife?' Marie Christine asked, glancing around curiously. I pointed Jan out.

'Oh, beautiful ... and very rich, I hear!' Marie Christine's voice carried clearly. The great and the good of Newport were riveted.

I assented in muffled voice, trying to hide my embarrassment.

'Well done, darling,' she said to me, chuckling loudly. 'I always knew you'd do well.'

Prince and Princess Michael stayed at the Pells' for a week. Every night some leading light of Newport gave a dinner for them, and on each occasion, Princess Michael kindly requested me to be seated at her table. My stock in that most aristocratic of America's vacation spots reached heights from which it never departed.

A little later in 1983 was still a time for political leaders in Newport. Vice President George H. W. Bush came for a fund-raising event prior to his successful run for the Presidency in the autumn and, for a joke, my Republican friends who had organised this invited me – a fervent supporter of the Democrats – to join them.

But I admired the Vice President and went along. Bush swept in with his Secret Service entourage and began to work the crowd. I was standing at the back of the room, a curious observer, sipping a glass of lukewarm champagne. Bush looked up, made eye contact with me, and came over to shake my hand. I was taken aback. I hadn't been prepared for this, but he, naturally assuming everyone was a potential donor, was nonstop motion on automatic pilot, glad-handing everywhere, joking,

was no need to worry, that I had telephoned one of Ted Heath's Special Branch protection officers at Scotland Yard and they were dealing with it. I replaced the phone and started to count slowly. I barely reached fifteen. The car engine roared back to life. It took off like a bat out of hell. I finished my drink and went to bed. I slept like a baby that night. My mind was made up.

It is true that I waited to tell Jan until after Ted Heath had left Newport that September. I couldn't see the point of ruining his visit with an enormous domestic row. In fact, as it turned out, there were hardly any rows, since Jan refused to believe I was serious.

'Don't be ridiculous!' she said, 'Why? We have the perfect marriage. Just be discreet, don't humiliate me, and do what you like.'

I really think she meant it, to a certain extent. But I was thirty-five years old, had no intention of spending the rest of my life in such circumstances, could hardly bear to be in the same room as Jan, and desperately wanted my freedom back as quickly as possible. Nothing was going to change my mind. My only concern was my son, both as regards his continued well-being and my future access to him.

I took a TWA flight to London the very next day. My brother met me at Heathrow to help me take my eight large bags to Eaton Place, the rest of my clothes could wait until I returned to visit John in two weeks' time. Even with a permanent ache in the pit of my stomach at the thought of him without me in New York, I have rarely been so relieved to be alone in my own little flat. Bliss. No staff, barely decorated, and hardly any furniture.

Jan, convinced that I would stay when I returned, for once did not call. Her tactic was to leave me in peace for the moment. But I began to settle in. I called my lawyers in New York to initiate legal proceedings. I called my old friends whom Jan had done her best to alienate. Full of excitement and optimism for the first time in what seemed a long time, I began to plan for the future.

Two weeks passed, and I duly returned for a few days, staying at the Surrey Hotel just across Madison Avenue from Jan's apartment. My priorities were to settle financial matters in the context of a divorce and to secure access to my son. There were few people I had any wish to bid goodbye. I knew the vast majority would follow the money and would want to be seen to take Jan's side. The New York press had already taken the lead in presuming, not very subtly, that I had only married Jan for her money. But I was deeply touched to receive a call from Norman Mailer, who wanted to take me to lunch. I was particularly touched because Norman was living in self-imposed exile in his house across the river in Brooklyn Heights while he wrote his murder mystery, *Tough Guys Don't Dance*, as quickly as possible to pay off an overdue, urgent income tax bill. He had confined himself to his writing for the last sixty days. We lunched at Veau d'Or, a favourite neighbourhood restaurant on 66th Street. Norman, dressed like a student in a zip-up windbreaker and chino trousers, entered through a side door to the customary murmur from other diners. He leaned on the table, stared earnestly into my eyes, and delivered his heartfelt advice.

'I've been married five times,' Norman could not have been more serious, 'and I want you to realise that you will drink a great deal for an extended period of time. You will get very drunk often, very often, as I did after each divorce. But I want you to remember that's okay. It's quite normal. I don't want you to worry about it. It won't mean you're becoming an alcoholic.'

I nodded my thanks gravely then stood up and hugged my dear friend tightly, not really knowing whether to laugh or cry, but full of love for the legendary hellraiser. We gently butted foreheads, a private sign of great affection.

'I'll see you next time you're back in town.'

Norman slipped off through the adoring crowd back to Brooklyn.

To my surprise, Winston Groom also tracked me down. He asked to meet for drinks to say goodbye. Again, I was touched. I had always been extremely fond of Winston. A modest, highly talented, gentle person who had served his country with distinction in the military during the Vietnam War. We met at Elaine's early one evening, and Winston confided that he too had decided to leave New York to return home to Alabama. He had a new idea for a book – the book that would become *Forrest Gump*. I have not seen Winston since, but have never forgotten his kindness.

I made a courtesy call on Jan's mother and stepfather to explain the situation. I was fond of them. Both had always been hospitable and considerate towards my father, my brother, and me. This became an emotional meeting for all three of us as they tried hard to change my mind. I felt for them when they finally resigned themselves to my decision with sad understanding.

I now had to concentrate on rationalising my business interests, as well as instruct my lawyers on the divorce. Both of these were simple processes. I sold my shares in the acquisition business to my partner Richard Berman who took over my midtown office with its lease liabilities. I did the same with my stake in Global Guarantees, which I sold to Rupert and Nigel at a decent profit. I was not happy in any case with the credibility of a new investor they had brought in. The latter turned out to be a convicted confidence trickster, posing as a representative of the Martini Foundation (which did not exist). Nevertheless, the business continued to be successful, eventually acquiring Film Finances to become the largest player in the sector. Rupert and Nigel exited some years later at a high price, taking their sales proceeds in stock in the buyer's company – this was tax efficient, but the buyer went bust and their shares became worthless. And although this was even more tax efficient, it really was most unfortunate.

The meeting with my divorce lawyers was simplicity itself. To their horror, I instructed them that I wished to waive all claims over Jan's financial and other assets, provided she did the same, and sought joint custody of John. Jan could also have the house in Newport, as long as she assumed the mortgage and I had use of it for two weeks every summer to be with John in the United States.

Since I was entitled to at least half of any increase in Jan's assets from the date of our marriage, my lawyers were mortified. They were expecting a performance bonus on top of their fees. The cash portion of Jan's capital, together with uplift on the value of her real estate, which we had negotiated from the Golding Trusts, amounted to many millions of dollars – and this was merely the guaranteed starting point. But I was determined to take nothing. To prove wrong all those, including the gossip columnists, who had crowed that I had married Jan for her money. In that sense, I was spectacularly successful; I never believed anyway that I would ever need a penny from Jan. But in another more important respect, I was completely wrong. I should have taken some cash and put it into a trust for John that would guarantee his future. It never occurred to me that his mother would have frittered away so much of her capital before her sixtieth year.

Jan's lawyers on the other hand couldn't believe their luck. Their client readily agreed to my terms. And as regards access to John, we also agreed that he would spend alternate Christmases and Easters with me in London, two weeks in Greece, and two weeks in Newport every summer (accompanied by a nanny), and alternate weekends at my hotel whenever I was in New York. In other words, joint custody. I explained all this to John, although he was too young still to understand. In addition, he was so used to my travel schedule that he would not notice anything had changed on a day-to-day basis, as long as I visited New York regularly. Such is the only advantage of an early divorce.

Whilst this settlement was very much in Jan's interests, I realised that she had not given up hopes of a reconciliation that easily, that she hoped the more reasonably she behaved, the more likely I was to have second thoughts. She was playing a 'long game' at this point. But more than satisfied with the progress I had made, I returned to my flat in London to embrace my freedom. To begin the next phase of my life.

And so, I slowly began to pick up the threads of my old bachelor life in London: lunches with the boys, connecting with old girlfriends, accepting invitations to dinner. I also began to spend alternate weekends in New York, where John would move into my hotel. Although I was not yet working full-time again, to fly out on a Friday evening and return overnight on Sunday evening was pretty exhausting. My friends thought this would be impossible to sustain when I did return to my career. It was difficult, but I'm proud to say that I kept it up until John was fourteen. At that point, Jan reluctantly agreed that John could live with me in England. I had arranged a place for him at Harrow School, which Jan accepted would be a superior education to that available to him in America. In addition, John wanted very much to take advantage of the opportunity. As it turned out, this was an enormous success. John had an outstanding school career – academically, in sports, and in popularity, making valuable friendships that have lasted decades. I was and am very proud of him. In particular, single handed, John resuscitated the moribund Palmerston Society, restoring it to an active forum of political debate. One of his first guest speakers was Ted Heath.

But that was later. In the meantime, Jan was becoming increasingly annoyed that I failed to show the expected signs of willingness for some sort of reconciliation. After a couple of months, my telephone in Eaton Place rang.

'Hi, Manoli, how are you?' My stomach turned over at sound of the unmistakable voice of Sidney Korshak.

'I'm okay, thank you Sidney,' came my reply, sounding far firmer than I felt, 'but not great, under the circumstances.'

'I'm sure, kid,' he rasped. 'Here's what I think you should do. It's time to go home. Go home. Go back to New York. Go back to your son, to your wife, your family. They need you. That's where you belong. Go home. You understand me?'

I took a deep breath. I had been expecting this. It was now or never.

'Sidney, you're kind to call,' I said, 'but I can't do that. Ever. I wouldn't be any use to either of them. I'm sure you understand.' I continued, 'I know of course something could happen to me. But if my son became an orphan, would it help him? I don't think so. Anyway, I'll just have to risk it, there's nothing else I can do.'

There was a long silence at the other end. I could hear my heart pounding in my ears.

'I guess not,' came the gruff reply. I swear I could detect a trace of laughter in the deep voice. 'Nothing you can do at all … but I guess you'll be okay, kid. Go carefully. Take care of yourself.' He rang off abruptly.

I put the phone down with a shaking hand. It would be all right. Deep down I had believed that the code Sidney operated by protected John, and thus by extension his father to a certain extent – unless I tried to hurt John or his mother, which Sidney knew I would never do. I had thought that, but I couldn't be sure until now. Sidney had only called because Jan asked him to. He had put me to the test, and I had passed.

I spent my first Christmas alone with my father and brother. I had been invited to a party on Christmas Eve, where I had bumped into an old girlfriend called Marianne Norton, who cheered me up tremendously, and whom I will always remember with great fondness. And then over lunch on Boxing Day, my dear friend Cliff Klenk invited me to join him in St. Moritz for a few days as a guest of Herbert and Eliette von Karajan. I had never met the great conductor, nor his wife Eliette, but Eliette was a close friend of Cliff's girlfriend Elizabeth, and the latter had been my guest on the *Spalmatori*. She kindly telephoned Eliette and obtained an invitation for me.

Accordingly, I arrived at St. Moritz in some style as a guest of the 'maestro', as everyone addressed him, and his wife. I actually saw little of the maestro, who was an intensely private man. In any case, he had to fly to Salzburg to conduct the orchestra there on New Year's Eve. We very much enjoyed Eliette's generous hospitality and spent much time walking in town (none of us were skiers) during the day. As house guests of Eliette, we were asked to several congenial dinners, at one of which I ran into Florence Grinda. She arranged for me to be invited to the New Year's Eve party which her friend Christina Onassis threw every year at the Chesa Veglia restaurant. This was the glamorous occasion one would expect. Full of beautiful, famous people, exquisitely dressed and bejewelled. I knew many of them, but not well. However, George and Lita Livanos went out of their way to show me great consideration which made me feel very much at home, as well as encouraging the other guests to make a particular effort with me. Christina asked me why I had left Jan, with genuine curiosity. I'm afraid I answered without thinking that it wasn't Jan's fault, but that it was difficult for most men to adjust to a wife that was far richer than them. I was trying to be a gentleman, but of course this was an extremely tactless reply given whom the question had been asked by. Christina just nodded graciously, with a wry, knowing smile.

In a buoyant mood I returned to London, looking forward to a fresh start to a new year with a clean slate.

CHAPTER ELEVEN

By Victories Undone

D URING OUR FILM VENTURE A FEW YEARS PREVIOUSLY, CARL Foreman had told me a fascinating story about an English acquaintance of his. Apparently, this man of noble birth had possessed a sixth sense, a gift, which enabled him to read other people's minds with startling accuracy. A gambler by nature, he utilised this gift in poker with great success. It made him all but invincible in those high-stake games to which he devoted most of his early adult life – an ancient title, a brilliant Oxford degree, inherited wealth, country estates, all notwithstanding.

Enormously popular among his group, his generosity would often cause him to waive the gaming debts of those who could not afford to lose. For ease of reference, I shall call him Jamie, as is his name in my novel.*

At the age of around forty, Jamie had a stroke. He recovered completely in a short time, but he had lost his gift and did not yet realise it. He began to lose. Heavily, steadily. Those whom he had counted as friends, those whom he had helped, took every advantage, consumed for years by a hidden jealousy of him. The fortune, the estates, everything began to melt away.

Finally, devastated and diminished, Jamie left England with a relatively small amount of money left. He immigrated to Australia. Here,

---

* Written with my co-author Raymond Lewis, *By Victories Undone*, see note 2.

fortuitously, he fell in love and married the wealthy widow of a well-known novelist. The marriage was a great success. Jamie worked hard to help his wife with her dead husband's literary estate. He unearthed significant writing royalties from all around the Far East. Several years passed, until one day he approached his wife. Promising there was no other woman involved, Jamie explained that he must return to England for some months, that he had unfinished business there, that he would take 50,000 pounds with him (a small fortune in the 1950s), and that he must go alone. His wife agreed without hesitation, understanding what had occurred.

Jamie's gift had returned in full force. He travelled to England, resumed his card playing, and won back everything he had lost. With ruthless determination, he then ruined those who had tried to ruin him. Jamie returned home to his wife, to Australia, and there they lived out their lives quietly, happily ever after.

This then was the kernel of the story that impressed me at the time. I have never forgotten it. Early in 1984, I wrote an outline of Jamie's story for a screenplay and left for New York to visit John, taking a draft with me. As always, I called Norman Mailer when I arrived in town. On my second night, I had dinner with him and Norris and asked him as a favour to read the outline. Two days after that, I arranged to have drinks with Norman at Le Club (a member's club) before his scheduled dinner there. Coincidentally, Norman's dinner was at the invitation of Del Coleman, Jan's first husband. Del was about to marry Karen Graham, the leading model of that moment, and he wanted to impress her by bringing her to dinner with Norman.

I duly arrived that evening at Le Club on time, at seven, to find that Del had appeared early and was already engrossed with Norman, who signalled to me that he would escape in a few minutes. Even more coincidentally, Jan then arrived. She was accompanied by Peter Kirwan-Taylor, a successful Englishman in the oil business, based in New York, and someone whom we all liked a great deal. Seeing me stranded alone at the bar, Peter, always a gentleman, asked me to join both him and Jan.

An offer kindly meant, but one which I declined. Patrick, the camp maître d', took one look at Del, Jan, and me in separate parts of the club, and had an attack of the vapours.

It was not long, however, before Norman joined me at the bar, to the extreme annoyance of Del.

He ordered a bourbon and ginger.

'I just want to tell you how great I think that story is,' Norman sipped his drink thoughtfully, 'but I don't think it's a screenplay. It's too good. It should be a novel. At least to start with.'

I was delighted, but taken aback, 'Norman, I really appreciate that, but … I can't write a novel.'

'Of course you can. I'll help you get started.' He was almost dismissive.

I could hardly believe my ears. Norman may have been one of my closest friends, but writing was a totally different kettle of fish. This was Norman's life. The one thing he took almost as seriously as his children. He had never helped or worked with anyone, firmly believing that his creative energy should be rationed for his own work. I was deeply touched.

'Okay,' I stammered, 'I'll get started when I get back home.'

Patrick interrupted, 'Excuse me Mr. Mailer, but Mr. Coleman wants to know when you can join him?'

'Tell him to fuck off. I haven't finished my drink.' Patrick had his second attack of the vapours. 'And by the way,' Norman continued, 'get that tramp story of yours in there. Use it, before I steal it.' He drained his drink, hugged me, and sauntered back to a visibly angry Del Coleman.

Jan glared at me from her table at the back of the room. I waved goodbye to my ex-wife, then to her first husband, and finally to a mightily relieved Patrick. I returned to my hotel grateful and excited by Norman's interest but not a little daunted at the prospect of writing a novel – even with Norman's help.

The 'tramp story' Norman had referred to was also a true one. I was at university, on the tube, on my way to a Roman law tutorial. I was on the Northern Line, headed for Tottenham Court Road, attempting to catch up on the last two lectures which I had skipped, when a boy of about twelve years of age wearing a smart prep-school blazer with grey flannel trousers boarded the train at the Oval. He sat immediately opposite me in the otherwise empty compartment. At the next stop an old man, clean and well shaven, but in ragged, tramp's clothing, boarded. He sat down next to the boy. Curiously, he wore a frayed Old Etonian tie around his collarless neck.

'Good morning, Jamie.' His tone was warm, his accent educated.

'Good morning, father.' The affection was reciprocated.

'I see you are well. Enjoying school, I trust ....'

All thoughts of Roman law fled from my mind. Open mouthed, I listened to a conversation between father and son that could have taken place over breakfast in a Victorian rectory. They chatted on. The train stopped at Waterloo.

'Wa-ter-loo,' the boy peered through the grimy windows, spelling it out hesitantly, 'that's a strange name.'

'Oh yes,' the tramp nodded, 'it's a little village in Belgium where there was a famous battle. The English, under the Duke of Wellington, defeated the French Emperor Napoléon there. In fact,' he continued proudly, 'your great grandfather D'Arcy commanded the Third Light at the time.'

Somehow, I managed to keep a straight face. A couple of stops later the tramp stood up.

'Well Jamie, I must be off,' he shook hands gravely with his son, 'see you next week. And give my best to your mother.'

This then was the anecdote I had recounted to Norman on my honeymoon that first weekend in Oxford. He had enjoyed it.

I took his advice. In my novel, *By Victories Undone*, the father becomes the grandfather, Jamie's grandfather. A baronet by the name of Clarence, he voluntarily takes to the streets, driven to madness by an even more powerful version of the gift for reading minds which Jamie has inherited. Clarence can read the future and it destroys him.

The reader may have noted that I usually refer to *Victories* as my novel, whereas my dear, departed friend Raymond Lewis is listed as co-author.

Indeed, Norman Mailer often used to wonder aloud why I would want to split royalties and writing credits. The answer is that the book would have been completely different had I written it without Raymond. Perhaps better, perhaps worse, but certainly different. The main story lines, the one lead character, were indeed told to me by Carl Foreman. Also, Norman's invaluable help was a result of his friendship with me. But all the subplots, all the other characters, and all the actual writing really were joint efforts with Raymond. It was a genuine, full-blown collaboration, during which Raymond put his practice at the Bar on hold for the duration. We were both proud of the result. I am frequently asked how one writes a book with someone else. In my experience it is extremely difficult – it would be much more common otherwise.

Raymond and I had been inseparable friends since law school, despite Jan's best efforts. We were as close as twin brothers, and since I have identical twin sons, I know a little about this. I could always start a sentence, Raymond could finish it, understanding exactly what was in my mind and vice versa. That was precisely how we did write together, whilst debating every word. We also argued strenuously over each subplot, improving them constantly we hoped. It was miraculous how ultimately the various strings of subplots came suddenly together, seemingly of their own volition, to form a seamless ending. To some extent, in the case of plot lines in particular, I suppose our creative partnership was no different to that of a longstanding screenwriting team. It was our modest ability to write not only dialogue, but prose together, which I believe is unusual.

In general, the advantage was that whenever one was having a bad or slow day, the other would normally compensate to pick up the pace. The disadvantage was that on those days when both of us were firing on both cylinders, compromises had to be made. Not so much in plot lines or subsidiary characters, but in the actual writing. There were times when this will have restrained prurient prose, but on other occasions potential inspiration was dumbed down. Nevertheless, there are several passages of which I am genuinely proud, and a final story which we were not alone in believing is quite a page-turner.

This foray into writing, however, has taken my current story slightly off course. Three years elapsed between my return to England and the launch party for *Victories*, so bear with me as I go back to detail some of the events of these years of newly regained freedom.

As this short chapter draws to a close, I have to pay tribute to two extraordinary human beings. First to our distinguished publisher and now my close friend, Naim Attallah CBE. The founder and chairman of Quartet Books is an erudite, lion-hearted, stylish man. Since being a young immigrant from Palestine, Naim has done it all: writer, interviewer, publisher, film producer, financier, former chief executive of the Asprey Group. A man of extraordinary energy and talents, now in his late eighties, he still shows no sign of slowing down. Thirty years ago, I gave him a draft of *Victories* one Friday. He told me his office would get back to me in a couple of weeks. Naim telephoned me himself two days later, the following Monday, to accept it. Apparently, he had been unable to put the book down all weekend. I will always be grateful for his faith in it, and I value greatly our subsequent friendship.

The final tribute, the last word on this subject, as so often, belongs to Norman Mailer. But what can you say when one of the most talented and celebrated writers of his generation – out of nothing but enormous affection for you – wants to help you write your insignificant book? He has left us now. How could I ever have thanked him enough? I did my best.

I want to share an early writing lesson from Norman. The prologue to the novel is set in a courtroom in which Jamie is on trial for his life. His legendary advocate has come out of retirement to defend him. We had written a few lines describing the nostalgia our ageing gladiator felt as he surveyed the arena from which he had withdrawn so long ago. When I went through the prologue with Norman, he had struck out those descriptive lines in red ink.

'No, no,' I protested, 'you don't understand. We want readers to understand his nostalgia. To realise how much the old lawyer has missed the smell of sawdust and greasepaint. How pleased he is to be back in a criminal court. Those lines are extremely important.'

'They're boring,' Norman said.

Then, with a quizzical look, he scrawled three words in their place. 'And he beamed.'

I was lost for words in more senses than one.

CHAPTER TWELVE

Normal Service Resumes

I CROSSED THE ATLANTIC EVERY OTHER WEEKEND TO VISIT JOHN. Otherwise, my London life took on a regular rhythm since my permanent departure from Jan and New York. In general, Raymond and I would meet at my apartment in Eaton Place every weekday morning. Here, we would plan, then write from eleven in the morning to two in the afternoon, and then break for lunch. This would usually take place at a restaurant, either Drones, Mimmo D'Ischia (Mimmo's), or San Lorenzo, or occasionally at the local pub. At four o'clock our secretary, Jill, would deliver the pages she had typed up from my barely legible longhand the previous day and collect that morning's work. We would spend the afternoon editing then sketching out new characters and subplots. By six-thirty, we were ready for our first drink of the evening, before we went our separate ways.

These hours may not sound particularly taxing, but the creative process, even on our lowly level, is a draining one. I speak with the experience of one who has regularly worked twelve-hour days in finance, and then hosted business dinners or negotiated transactions far into the night, for most of my life. Everyone is different of course. I found writing to be much more exhausting than business, but immeasurably more fulfilling. At least on a good day.

Nevertheless, the most important aspect is to 'put in the hours', working in any sequence, at any times that suit the author, but keeping up these hours day after day. Sometimes less than a page, perhaps only a sentence or two, perhaps nothing at all will be written. Other days, a whole chapter will spring forth almost fully formed. It took us two years. It should have been a year, but we learned this lesson the hard way, frittering away several months out of poor discipline and laziness. It didn't help that Raymond, at the age of thirty-four, had a serious heart attack in my flat halfway through. It took him six months to recover under the supervision of Tony Greenburgh, my brilliant doctor who fortuitously lived just around the corner.

In the evenings after work, I reverted to type, regularly playing poker with friends, but mainly pursuing the maximum possible number of beautiful girls in Annabel's or Tramp, my adventures as usual chronicled by the newspapers.

Despite this last minor irritation, life really was the most enormous fun in those years. I loved every moment, from writing hard to playing hard. One of the few upsides to having been married to Jan was the large and varied range of contacts that I had inherited from her, together with a certain social notoriety. Now an eligible single man, many invitations to all sorts of events ensued. And speaking of these, a particular telephone call came in at about four one afternoon.

I was due to attend Laurie Hunter's, one of my closest friends, fortieth birthday party that evening.

'Mr. Olympitis?'

'Speaking.'

'Claridge's Hotel here, Sir, please hold for Miss Streisand.'

Funnily enough, at the time, I didn't find this at all strange or unusual, although we hadn't had any contact since the South of France. I nodded silently.

She came on the line, 'Manoli, how are you?'

'Fine, Barbra. How are you? Welcome to London.'

'Yes, great,' she moved quickly along. 'You must be coming to my opening tonight? It's the premiere of *Yentl*.'

'Oh, I didn't realise. No, I'm afraid not.'

'What … but "tout Londres" will be there. I want you to come with me.' I think she was genuinely surprised I wasn't going. Perhaps she had put my name on an invitation list.

'Well, I'd love to,' I replied, 'but it's my best friend's fortieth party tonight, and I have to go.'

Silence. 'I don't think you understood. I said I'd like you to go with me. To accompany me.' The voice was becoming frosty.

'I'm really sorry, I would very much like to come, but I have to go to the birthday party,' I replied with regret, 'but how long are you in town for? Can I take you to lunch tomorrow? Or the day after?'

'Call me tomorrow.' Barbra hung up.

I still have no idea whether Barbra Streisand was asking me to go along as her date because she had been let down at the last minute, or as part of her group because of that evening at the Hotel du Cap two years before. I only know that at the time I thought it might just have been the former, since it was such a late telephone call, and she may well have thought I was coming in any case. The next morning the newspapers carried photographs of her with Steven Spielberg who must have committed a long time beforehand, so I have reluctantly dismissed the date theory. Laurie Hunter annoyingly told me that he wouldn't have minded, that I should have gone instead of going to his birthday party, but I must confess it never crossed my mind to do that. Much as I found Barbra attractive, a friend is a friend.

I duly called Claridge's the next day to invite her for lunch. Somewhat naïvely, I was surprised to be told she was too busy to talk to me, so I left a message. I tried again the following day, this time I was told that Miss Streisand had checked out. A year or two later, I went to one of her concerts, at the Albert Hall, I believe. She was magnificent. At the interval I sent her a note with my best wishes. When Barbra returned at the beginning of the second half, she chatted to the audience for a few minutes, mentioning she had friends amongst them. As she read out a short list of those friends who were there that evening, and specifically those from whom she had received a note, I braced myself for a suitable mention, but, sadly, no mention at all. I had obviously blotted my copy-book irretrievably. I have not been able to speak to or see Barbra Streisand since that phone call from Claridge's. A shame for me, perhaps a fleeting opportunity lost.

Some weeks after that telephone call, Norman and Norris Mailer came to London for the UK publication of *Tough Guys Don't Dance*. I arranged to give a dinner for them in the private room at Annabel's. Now, one of the joys of giving dinners for distinguished people is that you can ask them if there is anyone in particular they would like to invite. There almost always is, of course, and they are bound to be distinguished too. It is thus usually the case that you will meet new, interesting, well-known people who, although they may live in the same town, you would not have met otherwise. This was certainly the case that evening. The Mailers requested Sir Alfred 'Freddie' Ayer, the prominent philosopher, Shirley Conran, and Andrew Sinclair, the novelist, photographer, and publisher. They all accepted. To these I added, among others, Ted Heath, Mark and Marguerite Littman, as well as Edna O'Brien, whom I had met through Norman in New York, and my current girlfriend Caroline Kellett, a fashion editor at *Vogue*.

Dinner certainly was interesting, particularly for me, seated between Norris Mailer and Vanessa Ayer, Freddie's wife. I was enchanted by Vanessa, as was most of London society. Vivacious, funny, beautiful in an elfin, Audrey Hepburn way, she was sensational company. An electric energy and love of life seemed to crackle out of her – I was incredulous and much saddened to hear of her untimely death only a year or so later. All the guests were on good form that evening. The advantage of the private room at the original Annabel's was the convenience of being able to wander out on to the dance floor at will. Most of my guests enthu-siastically threw themselves into this as soon as coffee arrived, with the result that a great deal more champagne was consumed. The party was covered by *Portrait* magazine, and the photographs slightly bear this out.

We all left in great humour. This was only heightened for me by an extraordinary winning streak I achieved at the Clermont Club, where

Norman wanted to go afterwards. It wasn't until I was preparing to deal from the wooden baccarat shoe for the ninth time in succession that Shirley Conran, in a loud voice which cut through my mental bubble, exclaimed to Edna O'Brien, 'My God, at this rate he will have paid for the dinner,' breaking my concentration.

I looked up, slightly dazed. In fact, I was already way ahead of the cost of the dinner, but I knew instantly, in the way that gamblers do, that this was bad luck, the run was over, that this 'bank' was now jinxed. It wasn't Shirley's fault, she did not understand, but she did me a favour. I did not deal the next hand. I pulled my chips from the centre of the table, stood up, and passed the bank. It promptly lost. Time to go home. An unusually satisfactory evening. I purchased a new car with my winnings.

About six months before I gave up on my marriage to Jan, we had attended a charity dinner which was part of the Kennedy sisters' efforts to raise funds for their mentally disabled children's charity. Most of the leading cast of the film *Superman*, a current hit, were there in support, so, among other show-business people, I met Christopher Reeve, Gene Hackman, Margot Kidder, and Valerie Perrine. There was an immediate, mutual attraction between Valerie and myself, but I was married, she was nervous of Jan, and both of us ignored it. I'm sure we both then completely forgot about it until we met again in London nearly three years later at a friend's house over dinner.

A high-profile affair began which was to extend through the two following years in which I was writing *Victories*. By an extraordinary coincidence, Valerie turned out to be renting a flat at 34 Eaton Place – right next door to me. It wasn't long before she left that to move into number 36. My small dressing room was taken over by an enormous, circular, electric bulb-embedded, make-up mirror, which had obviously come straight off a film set; many pots of theatrical make up; and much exotic underwear, which spilled out of large, stuffed trunks that had to be clambered over in the hallway. It was all a mess. But for some time, quite a happy mess. A mess, however, which I did not then realise Valerie was taking far too seriously.

For the benefit of those who do not remember Valerie Perrine as an actress, or haven't come across any of her films, let me explain.

Valerie, a tall, spectacular blonde beauty with breasts that became legendary, had begun her career as a featured showgirl dancer in Las Vegas, behind acts such as Elvis Presley, Tom Jones, and Frank Sinatra. Spotted by a Hollywood talent scout, she had moved to Los Angeles in the early 1970s. Her breakthrough role was playing a porn star in the successful film of Kurt Vonnegut's bestseller *Slaughterhouse Five*. This won her a New York Film Critics Award for best supporting actress and a nomination for best actress. A celebrated naked *Playboy* centrefold and then cover followed. Valerie soon became the first American actress to appear nude on national television in the aptly named TV version of the off-Broadway black comedy by Bruce Jay Friedman, *Steambath*.

She was now an international sex symbol, but her role opposite Dustin Hoffman in the 1975 film *Lenny* turned her into a serious actress as well. Valerie received a Best Actress Academy nomination, a Golden Globe nomination, and won the Cannes Film Festival prize for Best Actress, as well as a BAFTA. Other major film roles followed in the late 1970s and early '80s,* but with the passing of time and the growing reputation of being 'difficult' on set, really good work was drying up.

Later, after our relationship had begun, I witnessed her being 'difficult'. I briefly visited the set of an unremarkable film called *Water*, which was being shot in St. Lucia with Valerie opposite Michael Caine. Called to the set at five in the morning, both stars had sat around for a full day with nothing to do because of technical problems with the equipment. Valerie was fuming by lunchtime and complained all afternoon to Dick Clement, the director, that they should have been released much earlier.

* Of note were *Superman I* (1978) as Gene Hackman's girlfriend, *The Electric Horseman* (1979) opposite Robert Redford, *Superman II* (1980) in the same role, and *The Border* (1982) with Jack Nicholson.

It was certainly annoying for everyone else, and to be fair, I'm sure other leading actresses would have thrown much worse tantrums. Whilst at the peak of her career, Valerie had upset powerful forces in the industry, who I believe painted her with this 'difficult' reputation as revenge.

On this occasion, Michael Caine had said little all day, quietly absorbed in his book. In the minibus on the way back to the hotel that evening, Valerie was still complaining.

He finally looked up from his book, 'Val,' Michael intoned in his nasal, staccato, voice, 'let me explain something. You know those times when we get to say our lines. Those times we enjoy. When we actually act? Or try to …'

Valerie looked surprised.

'Those times, Val, my darlin',' are for us. Just for us. And you know those times when we sit around all day. All bloody day. Doing absolutely nothing. Like today. Doing fuck all?'

Valerie nodded slowly, somewhat abashed.

'Those times are what they pay us for. And they pay us a lot. For doing nothing.' Michael returned to his book, message delivered.

But I digress again. By the time we had met in London, Valerie was taking an extended sabbatical from the film industry. At this point, she was in her late thirties, her figure was unchanged, her looks still ravishing. Whilst she had had several serious relationships – she was linked with Jeff Bridges and also the director George Roy Hill (*The Sting* and *Butch Cassidy and the Sundance Kid*) for some time – Valerie had never married and, to her deep regret, had no children. But she was highly popular. Her sense of fun, kind heart, and good humour in public at least, endeared her to many friends in London, where she had decided to settle for a while. We now became a regular 'item' as a couple around town, and my circle of friends and acquaintances began to expand exponentially further into the reaches of showbiz people on both sides of the Atlantic.

One week, Valerie decided that we should throw an informal Sunday night get together at Eaton Place, and that she would organise some interesting guests in addition to a small group of our closest friends. For help in this she turned to Astrid Wyman, a charming Swedish girl who was a good friend of hers and who had lived with Bill Wyman of the Rolling Stones as his common-law wife for many years. She had changed her name by deed poll and, although this relationship had ended, they remained close.

I had no idea who was coming that night. I had invited a few pals, including Michael Brandon and Glynis Barber of *Dempsey and Makepeace* fame,* organised the catering of food and drinks, and just waited for everyone to arrive. The guests invited by me arrived first. The party got started, and we began to have a jolly time. After about an hour, Astrid arrived with a couple of Valerie's other girlfriends and Bill Wyman, also in tow. He was extremely friendly and seemed a nice enough chap. Not long afterwards, Rod Stewart looked in, accompanied by a sensational blonde model. He had a quick drink, was very polite to everyone, and left. My friends were impressed by Bill and Rod, as well as by Michael and Glynis, and were enjoying themselves uproariously when the doorbell rang for the last time.

The last two guests arrived. Mick Jagger and David Bowie sauntered in together, literally arm in arm, both of them smiling and relaxed. I don't remember much detail after that, except that they mingled and chatted with everyone as if we had all been friends for years. But I can vividly remember the high point of the party: Mick and David, as I was calling them by now, were improvising and simultaneously singing bits of the odd song every now and then. Suddenly, they switched into a fluent routine in perfect unison, singing together while dancing up and down my cleared hallway in precise steps. They were performing an impromptu rehearsal of 'Dancing in the Street', a song and dance routine they subsequently performed to great acclaim for the Live Aid Concert the following year. It became a number-one hit for them worldwide. I

---

* Originally friends of Valerie's, Michael and Glynis became friends of us both after they confided in us about their secret relationship at Michael's birthday party that year. I later made a speech at their wedding, and they spent some of their honeymoon with me in Greece.

realise now they must have been in the midst of recording this at the time, but no one had yet heard their version. To hear and see it in such proximity, under such circumstances, was a terrific moment, of which my friends still remind me.

∾

Valerie now began to accompany me to New York on my trips to see John. Always good with children, she was an eternal child at heart herself, and the two of them got on well. More usefully, Jan, impressed by the American movie-star syndrome, behaved herself around Valerie. Furthermore, she had met Charles Minot Amory IV whom she decided would be her next husband. Happy for the moment, she wanted us to be friends and have a civilised approach to parenting John. I was delighted and relieved – and very stupid to think this would last, as we shall see.

In New York, I introduced Valerie to Norman and Norris Mailer. For Norman it was practically love at first sight. He also admired Valerie's work as an actress to the extent that he was convinced she would be perfect for the female lead in the film of his recent bestseller *Tough Guys Don't Dance*. His great friend Ryan O'Neal had agreed to play the male lead. Norman had written the screenplay so that was all fine, but the problem for Valerie was that Norman would direct. Much as she respected him as a writer, she was totally dismissive of his directorial abilities. Norman understood, indeed accepted this. He pressed me to persuade her but gave up when he saw that I had no more chance than him. Reluctantly, he gave the part to Isabella Rossellini who was at the beginning of her acting career. He hoped it might be her first break. Sadly, Valerie was proved right. The film, whilst it contained decent performances by Ryan and Isabella, was rather disjointed and lost its way with both the critics and the public, sinking with little trace.

Valerie knew all the show people in New York, and we enjoyed many evenings together on these visits. I remember we took Brenda Vaccaro and Ann Turkel (recently divorced from Richard Harris) to dinner at Sam's after the opening night of *The Odd Couple* on Broadway. Sam's was the 'hottest' place in New York at that time, and Ann had heard the Rolling Stones were coming. She was wrong, but over dinner we were joined by Christopher Reeve; Robert De Niro, Al Pacino and Madonna, on the table next door were introduced to us.

One of the best introductions for me however, was at first sight, a rather less glamorous one.

Valerie was always conscious of her image, and whenever there was insufficient time for the lengthy process of getting ready to venture outside, Valerie would resort to some form of disguise to remain anonymous. A few days after dinner at Sam's restaurant, we left the Mark Hotel around midday with the vague intention of eating brunch somewhere. Valerie not exactly disguised but with no make-up, a khaki rain hat pulled low over her forehead, a voluminous khaki raincoat draped around her body, was safely unrecognisable.

Hunched against a sharp, chilly, New York spring shower, we wandered down Madison Avenue. There were few pedestrians braving the weather that late morning, but a solitary tramp was shuffling along towards us, his filthy clothes damp, he looked distinctly smelly. As he passed, I braced myself for the unavoidable, pungent moment. Instead, I was taken aback by a cheery 'Hi, Valerie' in a familiar voice, followed by a grin and the wink of a piercing blue eye. Paul Newman, in a real disguise, had just passed by. 'Hi, Paul,' had been Valerie's poker-faced reply, followed by a jab in my ribs to keep me quiet.

I was to have the privilege of meeting the undisguised Paul Newman over a drink at a charity event soon afterwards. Valerie knew him well through her relationship with George Roy Hill, one of Newman's closest friends, he had directed him in both *The Sting* and *Butch Cassidy and the Sundance Kid*. Newman had always been one of my screen heroes, but in real life, I realised he was a great deal more. We all know Paul Newman was a highly talented, powerful actor; he was also an extraordinarily warm, amusing, intelligent, and caring person. He founded a charitable food company specialising in a range of sauces and dressings under the name of Newman's Own. To this venture he dedicated an enormous amount of time and energy. To date, this has contributed over 500 million dollars to worthy causes. It was a privilege to have met him.

At this point, relations between Jan and me had warmed to the extent that we could now agree workable arrangements as regards John's summers. These extended to my occupying the house in Newport for about ten days, whenever Jan went to the South of France, and John joining me and my father on Kalymnos for two weeks in August. In the early years, John was always accompanied by his English nanny, Barbara. I was careful never to have girlfriends around during these stays, since Jan would have felt her relationship with John threatened. It was a measure of the respect she had for Valerie, however, that she did not object to Valerie staying with me and John in Newport. Here, Valerie caused some amusement at the Beach Club when young children, recognising her from *Superman*, would frequently run after her into the sea shouting joyfully that she had saved Superman's life.

Life with Valerie in London was equally enjoyable, and we and various friends made the most of the wide array of venues and connections that great city had to offer. I had first met Margaux Hemingway in New York in early 1980, through Jan of course. Margaux too had just married a French filmmaker called Bernard Faucher. Although still only in her mid-twenties then, Margaux's brilliant but short career as a supermodel was effectively over, and she was now attempting to build upon her recent success as an actress in the cult film *Lipstick*. Her looks were as wonderfully striking as ever. A fabulous six-foot brunette, Margaux had large brown eyes under full, dark, boyish eyebrows, set in a wide face with sharp cheekbones. It was the face of a beautiful, athletic, all-American girl-next-door, and all of America had fallen in love with it when she was discovered at nineteen years old. She was a thoroughly popular person in New York, friendly, approachable, sparkling, with a genuine air of unspoilt innocence. Although her voice was a decidedly unusual mix of Lauren Bacall and Donald Duck, this served only to heighten her attractive individuality. Margaux seemed to lead such a charmed life, so full of laughter, fun, and privilege, as a result of her famous grandfather, that only her closest circle was aware of her periodic dark moods and depressions, amplified by continual financial instability.

I was extremely fond of Margaux and liked Bernard. We all became fast friends, dining and partying in New York a great deal, holidaying together in Newport and Jamaica. I missed Margaux when I moved back to London, but her marriage, then under heavy financial strain, broke up soon after mine, and having met David Ford through our mutual friend Jubby Ingram (who worked for Naim Attallah), Margaux moved to London too. I was delighted. I saw a great deal of her, David, and Jubby. Margaux and I remained close until her untimely death in 1996, aged only forty-two.

However, that tragedy had yet to unfold, and one autumn day in 1985 when about to order lunch with Valerie and Margaux at Harry's Bar, I was approached by an elegant Middle Eastern lady of a certain age who was being entertained by Nigel Dempster at a nearby table. Nigel came over to introduce us. Her name was Leila, she was Jordanian, her demeanour quiet and courteous. She shook hands with me gravely, and asked to be introduced to Valerie and Margaux, both of whom she apparently admired.

I invited her and Nigel to sit with us for a few moments. Leila explained that she had just opened a Jean-Paul Gaultier boutique shop on Hay Hill nearby (Gautier was just beginning to make his name) and that she believed a certain amount of sophisticated promotion was desirable. To this end, she invited me to bring both girls to the shop later in the afternoon: she would like to invite them to each choose an outfit for themselves free of charge, provided that they were prepared to wear it on one or two occasions, high-profile enough for them to be photographed. Valerie, always an independent spirit, demurred, while Margaux, who these days was happy to take an opportunity that came her way, accepted with alacrity.

Deep into the afternoon, we wandered down to Hay Hill in the company of our new friend. I watched with curiosity as the girls examined the various racks of clothes in their very different ways, Valerie with an air of bored indifference, Margaux with purposeful concentration. In the end, Valerie couldn't find anything she liked, so Margaux gleefully chose two outfits.

We were all moved into Leila's office for tea while the labels were removed and the clothes were folded and wrapped. This small, comfortable room was remarkable only in that it was dominated by a large oil portrait of King Hussein of Jordan dressed splendidly in full military uniform. An assistant poured tea, and Leila chatted animatedly in Arabic with someone she had just telephoned. This conversation suddenly paused. Leila held out the telephone receiver to Margaux.

'His Majesty the King of Jordan would like to speak to you,' she announced grandly.

A bewildered Margaux took the phone. 'Hi, King,' she said huskily, with absolutely no idea of the impropriety of this form of address.

I was finding this hilarious, until I heard the unmistakable voice of King Hussein; the way he ignored Margaux's naïve lack of formality was impressive. They chatted for a few minutes before Leila took back the telephone and the call ended shortly afterwards. She then announced that His Majesty had invited us all to be his guests at Petra the following weekend.

Most generous though this invitation was, Valerie and I had plans and all three of us politely declined. We exchanged telephone numbers, thanked Leila, and left. It had been an interesting afternoon. Although I suspect even more interesting for Margaux. She was not contactable the following weekend, and when I next had dinner with her, I could not help noticing the new jewel-encrusted Cartier watch on her tanned left wrist.

∽

Late in 1985, Raymond and I decided to undertake some final rewrites of our novel before sending manuscripts to potential publishers. Valerie had accepted the female lead in a new CBS sitcom opposite Harvey Korman, the first episode to be directed by Steve Martin, so she was back in her Los Angeles house. She persuaded us to come out, stay with her, and rewrite by the pool while she worked on set. I was happy to do this and had many interesting times with her at various industry functions, but was less happy to agree to a suggestion made by her press agent that we pretend we were engaged to be married as part of a publicity drive to promote her new show. It did seem ungracious not to go along with it, despite my unease. But the problem with an actress as good as Valerie is that after playing a role like this for a short time, the part becomes their reality – particularly if the press keeps mentioning it, and particularly if she secretly wanted it to be true in the first place. I was very aware it could all end in tears, but shrugged off my forebodings for the time being. Although I have to admit that these were somewhat magnified by the presence of a 0.38 revolver which Valerie, a good Texan girl, kept fully loaded in a shoulder holster that hung from her bedpost every night.

I should say at this point that it is impossible to live in the Beverley Hills area without constantly coming across famous people – whether at the gas station or the supermarket, let alone at dinner parties if you are escorting a well-known actress. After a while, this becomes commonplace and everyone gets used to it. With familiarity comes the ability to recognise the frailties of our celluloid heroes, and whilst this does not necessarily breed contempt, it does bring about a realisation that they are human beings after all. However, every now and then there can be a moment of fairy dust which leaves you breathless, wondering if it has really just taken place. One such moment happened to me at a party Alana Stewart gave at the house she had shared with Rod Stewart before their divorce and which she was about to vacate. It was a winter night soon after New Year.

Alana was a well-known, popular hostess. I did not know her, but she was a good friend of Valerie's who took me along. There must have been close to one hundred guests. The place was packed with stars. Legends with well-preserved faces and flatteringly cut dinner clothes from Old Hollywood, alongside seriously beautiful people currently reaching the peak of their fame from the younger group. I felt as if on a film set, set in an unreal world. This strange sensation was heightened, although I had never felt particularly tall at six foot one before, by the feeling that I was towering over everyone – diminutive in stature as actors often are. I had arrived with Valerie and with George Hamilton, who was escorting Elizabeth Taylor that evening. I had seen quite a lot of both George and Elizabeth separately over the previous weeks and was on good terms with them. George I had known quite well from London, Elizabeth liked Valerie and had been kind to me since my arrival in Los Angeles. She was not only still beautiful, but also great company, possessing an irreverent, salty sense of humour combined with a refusal in private to take herself at all seriously. I found myself seated between Elizabeth and the writer Jackie Collins, who couldn't have been nicer. Opposite me was Berry Gordy, the founder of Motown Records, a quiet, seemingly shy man, with a breathtakingly beautiful black girl next to him who may or may not have been his wife, but to whom he whispered constantly. Valerie was placed at Alana's table, next to Jack Nicholson.

Everyone was having a jolly time when the mood was lifted even more by the appearance of a choir singing Christmas carols from the minstrels' gallery that ran around the enormous dining room. Soon, all the guests were enthusiastically singing along, myself included. 'Hark The Herald Angels Sing' turned into 'O Come All Ye Faithful', but this had a more muted accompaniment since the choir was singing the Latin version of 'Adeste Fidelis', the words to which were not known to most of the guests. However, five years of Christmas services at my old school King's in Canterbury Cathedral had taught me well. I continued to belt out the Latin words, but because of the much softer guest involvement, I could make out a well-known, in fact a legendary, male voice singing fluently from directly behind me. For some time I did not turn around. I couldn't place the voice but, knowing only that it belonged to a very famous singer, I thought it would be uncool to face the other way and stare. At the end of the carol however, I did slowly look round with exaggerated casualness to be confronted by the smiling face of Gene Kelly. He put out his hand in the friendliest way. I shook it perhaps a little too energetically as he introduced himself. I'm afraid what I did after that was the height of uncool. I am mortified every time I think of it.

'Gene,' I asked earnestly, 'Singin' in the Rain?'

He looked nonplussed, 'What?'

'Singin' in the Rain,' I repeated, my eagerness overflowing. 'Just one verse … together … the two of us?'

An expression of incredulity crossed Gene Kelly's face, 'You have to be joking.' The words came out slowly, with the emphasis on the word 'joking'.

And so, finally embarrassed, I turned away to meet the pitying stares of my neighbours at dinner. I hung my head, ashamed of myself. But then suddenly, totally unexpectedly, quietly, came light, lilting tones from behind me, 'Doo – de – doo – de – do – doo – de – do … I'm singin' in the rain …'

I swung around in amazement. Gene Kelly had a broad grin; his eyes were fixed on a point high on the ceiling.

'Just singin' in the rain …'

I joined in excitedly. No one further than ten feet away could hear us.

'It's a glorious feeling, I'm happy again.'

Gene Kelly stopped abruptly and looked directly at me.

'Okay, kid. Show's over.'

'Thank you, so much … one day I will tell my grandchildren,' I was ridiculously grateful by now.

'No one will remember it by then.' He waved me away kindly.

'My God, Manoli. That was brave! I wouldn't have dared ….' Liz Taylor was doubled up with laughter, clapping her hands like a little girl. 'Amazing you got him to do that.'

It was certainly a moment to remember.

Not as noteworthy, but more revealing, was another moment a few days later at George Hamilton's house. George had bought Charlie Chaplin's original, neoclassical-style mansion in Beverley Hills and was throwing a drinks party to celebrate Catherine Oxenberg's birthday. She was appearing with him in the TV series *Dynasty*. I was standing amongst a group of people who were chatting animatedly together over a delicious rum punch on one side of the swimming pool. Greco-Roman statues interspersed with pine and eucalyptus trees surrounded the pool. It was close to a full moon that night, the air was scented, the moonlight glistened on the water, frogs and crickets croaked and chirruped.

'Jeez, isn't this beautiful.'

Another familiar, famous voice. I turned. Clint Eastwood was towering over me – for a change – with his partner Sondra Locke beside him. I had never met him. He introduced himself gravely and introduced me to Sondra. He stared around the moonlit pool, completely entranced.

'So glamorous. Can't you just imagine Hedy Lamarr or Carole Lombard coming out from behind one of those statues? What a time that must have been,' he mused, in wonder upon the golden days of Hollywood.

And to me, this was a revelation. There he was. Clint Eastwood. A seriously nice man who happened to be the biggest film star in the world at that time. And he was just as star struck as the rest of us. Entranced since childhood by that magical celluloid world which had drawn him into its comforting embrace. A world to which he now, in turn, drew in another generation.

Rewrites of our novel were complete. I sent the final draft to Norman Mailer in the hope that he could find us an agent, which indeed he did. One of the most powerful talent agencies, ICM Partners, signed us up, and the search for a publisher began. In the meantime, it was time for me to earn some money again, and for Raymond to return to the criminal bar. It was time to bid farewell to the sweet escapism of Beverley Hills' show business and Los Angeles. Time to get back to London, to reality. After a tour of Disneyland and Universal Studios, I took John back to his mother in New York, continuing on to London. Valerie would join me when she could.

CHAPTER THIRTEEN

Back to Work

I HAD JUST STARTED TO CONTACT MY LONDON BANKING FRIENDS and the usual headhunters when I received an unexpected call from Tony Constance. Tony was my old boss at Manufacturers Hanover. A senior City figure in merchant banking, he had just been hired as group chief executive of Aitken Hume International, the publicly quoted financial services company, replacing Tim Aitken. The latter, a grandson of Lord Beaverbrook, had founded and built the group together with his politician cousin, Jonathan Aitken MP, about whom more is explained below. The group now consisted of two banks with funds under management of two billion pounds, a life insurance company, and a property company that had been created by another cousin, Johnny Kidd. All three cousins were directors, Jonathan the Chairman and Tim the CEO.*

Of late, expansion had stalled, the share price was sliding, a bitter falling out had taken place amongst the cousins. Tim Aitken and Johnny Kidd stormed off the board and out, quickly followed by Prince Michael. The life insurance company was acquired shortly before the boardroom schism, through a share issue largely underwritten and subsequently taken up by Wafic Saïd, a personable Syrian businessman with links to the Saudi royal family. As a result, Wafic now owned twenty-three per cent of Aitken Hume. A friend of Jonathan Aitken's – who was himself

---

* The non-executive directors included Prince Michael of Kent, Sir Kenneth Cork (a former Lord Mayor), and Stuart Graham (a former chief executive of Midland Bank).

well-connected to the Saudis – Wafic was officially an adviser to British Aerospace for whom he acted in their successful bid to supply British-built Tornado fighter aircraft to the Saudi government in the first of a multi-phased programme. This was known as the Al Yamamah programme; it was to be worth scores of billions of pounds to the British government over the next twenty years.

Wafic Saïd was subsequently labelled an 'arms dealer' by the press, because he undoubtedly became a very rich man in that process. Additional rumours concerning the vast commissions normally connected with such dealings would extend beyond him and Jonathan Aitken to the Thatcher family, in the person of Mark Thatcher, but no wrongdoing was ever proved on the part of any of them. Certainly, the British taxpayer profited handsomely. Some years later, Wafic Saïd was to make a generous bequest of 100 million pounds to Oxford University to found the Saïd Business School. He always maintained that he had never so much as 'dealt in a penknife'. I can't help believing that there was an anti-Arab bias among the British press at that time. After all, if an establishment British figure had been representing British Aerospace, I doubt whether he would have been described as an arms dealer, no matter how much money he had made for himself. But I suppose that goes with the territory.

In any event, this was the heated and highly charged atmosphere surrounding Tony Constance's appointment to succeed Tim Aitken. The immediate task was to eliminate the annual operating losses, calm the anxiety of the Bank of England, and then continue to expand the group. For this, Tony was seeking a deputy he could trust. Whilst eminently capable in a traditional banking environment, Tony was new to the controversial, freewheeling, and entrepreneurial culture of Aitken Hume. He considered me to have sufficient 'street smarts' through my North American experiences to be able to help. Excited by a new challenge in a different arena, I accepted Tony's offer and joined Aitken Hume under him as group managing director.

Hardly had I moved into my new office when we were subjected to a hostile takeover bid by a special purpose vehicle called Tranwood, an entity which was controlled by Nick Oppenheim, an ambitious financier of the moment. This takeover bid was to be bitterly fought out in the glare of unwelcome press attention which, as usual, touched upon my private life.

In retrospect, Aitken Hume seems to have been a magnet for colourful characters in many respects. The permanent cast of Wafic Saïd, Jonathan Aitken, and Lee Ming Tee was joined briefly by the hulking presence of Robert Maxwell. Throughout the several weeks of the hostile Tranwood bid, either Tony Constance or I would chair a Defence Committee meeting each morning at eight. The attendees would be our lawyers, Simmons & Simmons, our merchant bankers, Morgan Grenfell, and our PR advisor, Tim Bell (later Lord Bell) of Bell Pottinger. Tim was famously colourful – funny, irreverent, brilliant, larger than life. He was Margaret Thatcher's favourite advertising man; his slogan 'Labour Isn't Working', set above a long line of unemployed, for a poster campaign, had helped the Conservatives win the 1979 general election. Tim became a staunch friend, and for every subsequent company I managed throughout my career, I would appoint his firm.

Together, all of us would examine the various moves from the opposition and plan an appropriate response. At the end of one of these meetings, Guy Dawson of Morgan Grenfell took a phone call from his office and drew me aside. Another of their clients, in the large shape of Robert Maxwell, had contacted them. He wished to meet with me to discuss the possibility of his becoming a 'white knight' for us. He knew that I would be attending his son Ian's thirtieth birthday at the family home in Oxford that very evening and would have a quiet word with me there.*

Although Ian Maxwell was a friend, and his father's fortunes – he had a few years earlier become proprietor of the *Daily Mirror* – were riding

---

* For those who have not come across the expression a 'white knight', in this context it is a person or persons to whom the board or the shareholders of a public company agree to surrender control at a reasonable price per share, in order to avoid the company being forcibly acquired by a less-welcome entity at a lower price.

high in the late 1980s, I shared the general distaste in the City for Robert Maxwell. However, my opinion was not important. What counted was the position of the rest of my board, and in particular of Wafic Saïd as the largest individual shareholder. It was quite clear to me by this time that, although we believed we would defeat Tranwood, it would be a close-run thing. It could well be that a better price could be extracted from Maxwell now. Tony convened a board meeting to obtain a decision, and we were unsurprised to be told by Wafic, Jonathan, and the others that they had no interest in recommending Robert Maxwell's approach to the body of shareholders at virtually any price. Armed with this, I set out for Oxford and a birthday party which I realised would now hold little joy for me.

Halfway through dinner, Robert Maxwell loomed up beside my seat. I had not met him before.

'Let's go outside for a walk,' he barked. He pushed me towards a back door.

It was a cold night in February and frozen snow lay on the ground. Neither of us were wearing overcoats, but with his bulky frame he was clearly warmer than me. I was extremely cold. With short, vigorous steps, Maxwell proceeded to frogmarch me around the estate.

'You know what I want to discuss?' I nodded.

'Well, you're going to lose. Get used to it. You're going to lose big time. Get it!' I said nothing.

'You've heard of my friend, David Stevens? He runs a lot of money. Several billion. A fund manager called Montagu Investment Management – MIM. He's also now chairman of the Express Newspaper Group.' I just nodded again. I hadn't met him (but more of Stevens ten years later).

'We're in this together. We plan to inject your funds under management into MIM. We'll sell everything else. We don't need any of your staff. They will go too. But if you help us, there'll be a good spot for you with us. One where you can make some proper money. Well? What do you say?'

'Mr. Maxwell,' I replied rather weakly in the face of this torrent, 'my board and I are very flattered by your interest in our company, but I'm afraid...'

'Afraid! You're afraid!' He began to shout, 'You bloody well should be afraid, you bloody idiot. You're going to lose. All of you. We'll fire Constance. And you will have no job either, unless you come in with us. And if you don't, you'll never get to run another public company again. I can guarantee you that!'

I was becoming enraged despite the temperature. 'Mr. Maxwell, I'm sorry,' my voice as cold as the weather, 'we had a board meeting today. I am instructed to thank you for your interest, but my board does not wish to accept your kind offer to be a white knight.'

'Doesn't accept my offer!' He was positively bellowing now, his steps quickening in agitated frustration. 'You haven't even heard my offer yet, you fucking idiot! Nor have your fucking idiotic board!'

'Mr. Maxwell,' I stopped walking abruptly, so that he did the same, 'our board will not consider recommending an offer from you, unless it is at a very favourable price. Besides,' I added mildly, 'we are confident that we will win. However, if you do have a favourable price in mind for our shareholders, please state it now.'

Naturally, Maxwell refused.

'Win! You'll win? No fucking chance, you fucking idiots,' he spat.

Quietly, politely, I excused myself and found my way back to the house. I made my excuses to Ian, who nodded sombrely, and I left to return to London. I never saw Robert Maxwell again. Ian is still a friend, as is his brother Kevin. Aitken Hume survived the takeover bid by two per cent of the shareholder vote. Thereafter, we were able to turn the nine million-pound loss into a three million-pound profit the following year. We expanded the banking side with a couple of acquisitions and an arrangement to look after some of IMG's best-known golf stars, whilst selling the loss-making life insurance company. Along the way, Tony Constance resigned over the failure of the board to support him in an agreed acquisition of another bank, Rea Brothers. By now, a Chinese entrepreneur based in Hong Kong called Lee Ming Tee had acquired twenty-five per cent of our stock in the fallout from the failed Tranwood bid.

Lee Ming Tee was a somewhat mysterious character with strong connections to mainland China. Wafic had raised his stake to twenty-five per cent in response. These two now effectively controlled Aitken Hume. Both were non-executive directors, both controversial characters. It was unclear why Lee Ming Tee had bought his shares, and much speculation was focused on a potential relationship between him and Wafic outside Aitken Hume. Tony felt passionately that the Rea Brothers merger made enormous sense, that this was a unique opportunity for a quantum leap of growth. To him, the failure of the board to support this plan confirmed his suspicions that the controlling shareholders – with the support of Jonathan Aitken – had a business agenda of their own which did not necessarily coincide with the apparent interests of the company.

I tried my best to dissuade Tony, but he was adamant that he must leave, and by now his personal relationships with the non-executive directors and the chairman were in tatters. Nevertheless, in an honourable manner, Tony asked me not to leave with him, at least for the time being, concerned that someone should hold the fort, that our good work not be wasted, and that the small shareholders not suffer a consequent loss. I agreed. In any event, I was not convinced that there was something necessarily sinister in the board's refusal to back the merger, although it was obvious the major shareholders did not wish to relinquish control of the company at this stage. A few months later I was appointed chief executive in Tony's place, still enthusiastic to do my best but wary of limitations that might be placed upon me by the board. Nevertheless, in the meantime, at the age of thirty-nine, I was the youngest chief executive of a significant, fully listed financial services company in the City. This was a time when it was common for men in their late fifties and early sixties to hold such positions.

The majority of the colourful characters that came and went were connected to Jonathan Aitken.* We did business with some of them. Most would remain valuable contacts for years afterwards. Our board had been enlarged, and meetings were a little calmer with the addition of Sir Peter Gadsden, chairman of PPP Healthcare Foundation, but they were still capable of being the scene of sudden, quite dramatic rows. Jonathan Aitken would normally struggle to preside in an unbiased manner, favouring as always Wafic Saïd's point of view. In addition, Jonathan's relationship with the truth was often stretched, foreshadowing his conviction for perjury some years later. This lack of consistent support from my chairman made a coherent strategic plan extremely difficult for me to develop, let alone execute – as Tony had predicted. However, I have to say that, whilst I could rely on Jonathan only to let me down when the going got tough in board meetings, I was, and still am, genuinely fond of him. I was sorry for his later disastrous wrongdoing, and I maintained contact both immediately before and after his time in prison.

During these board meetings, there were often hilarious moments of levity that followed quite serious disagreements. On one such occasion, an emotional Wafic Saïd accused the chief executive (me) of 'putting his own interests before the company's', because of a recent corporate acquisition I wished to retain that he considered too dilutive to the shareholders – particularly in relation to his own shareholding. In retrospect, he was right about the dilution principle. But I became enraged at this attack on my integrity; Jonathan of course did not even try to defend me, pretending he hadn't heard the remark, and it took Sir Kenneth Cork to call for the lunch interval early to calm tempers down.

'In case you foreigners don't know,' Kenneth said patronisingly to a glowering Wafic and to me, 'it is a custom of British public companies

---

* These included Edward St. George, the Bahamian multimillionaire investor who owned ten per cent of our stock, who took me to lunch several times to bombard me with his ideas on increased funding for expansion. Sir Edward du Cann MP, chairman of Lohnro plc; Mark McCormack, the founder of IMG; Aziz Syriani, CEO of the Saudi Olayan family group, were among many others.

that we never discuss business over lunch. At this rate we will all get indigestion.'

Quietly, the board filed downstairs to the dining room, even desultory conversation muted until after the main course. At that point, in an attempt to break the ice, I asked Jonathan whether a debate in the Commons the previous day – preceding the passage of an Act of Parliament under which a husband was now legally capable of raping his wife – had been interesting or spirited in any way. As Jonathan gratefully launched into a lengthy description, Wafic began to turn purple. After a few more minutes, now a bright shade of puce, he started to stand up.

'Wafic! No! No! Control yourself, please!' Kenneth Cork anticipated a resumption of the furious boardroom row with me.

'But why? Why!' Wafic shouted, ignoring him, practically apoplectic. 'Why, would ANYONE want to rape their WIFE?!'

He sat down again suddenly. There was a momentary silence. It was broken by my laughter, now with tears streaming down my face. I went over to Wafic, held my arms open, shaking with mirth. We hugged each other warmly, friends again.

The four elderly English directors present stared, amazed at this unedifying display of emotion by their foreign colleagues. The humour of Wafic's remark completely passing them by.

To return to our chairman, Jonathan Aitken, briefly: he was an attractive character with an interesting background. In many ways, Jonathan was a typical product of the Establishment. A great nephew of Lord Beaverbrook, the son of a distinguished Conservative MP, he had been educated at Eton and Oxford. Jonathan was articulate, intelligent, good looking, but fond of the finer things of life without the inherited means to indulge them. Highly ambitious, he deployed his advantages determinedly, with perhaps a little too much charm. He began to depart from his Establishment credentials.

Early success as a journalist on the family newspaper created a certain reputation for fearless foreign reporting in Africa, but the publication of his first book, *The Young Meteors*, earned him considerable opprobrium amongst his peer group, who felt betrayed by some indiscretions about their personal lives which it contained, and they never quite trusted him again.

Elected to Parliament in 1972 at the age of thirty-four, Jonathan appeared destined for a dazzling political career until he fell out of favour with Mrs. Thatcher, apparently over the ending of his engagement to her daughter.* Backbench politics, a biography of Richard Nixon, and the business of making money became Jonathan's work-life priorities. The founding of Aitken Hume was an important aspect of this, as was the controversial acquisition of TV-am – a very public mess which included Anna Ford throwing a glass of wine into Jonathan's face in a celebrated incident at a Chelsea drinks party.† A few days later, she and Angela Rippon began proceedings against TV-am, which were settled out of court. Jonathan, who as an MP could not continue as chief executive under the broadcasting legislation anyway, gave way to Timothy Aitken.

In the meantime, Aitken Hume had obtained a public listing, becoming an increasingly important player in financial services. But after Wafic Saïd had invested, after the Tranwood takeover attempt, and after the entrance of Lee Ming Tee, suspicion lingered amongst certain sections of the financial press that the primary purpose the company now served was to provide a forum in which some of its directors might also discuss controversial commercial transactions between themselves in unrelated areas, such as armament transactions in the Middle East and Far East.

These suspicions were heightened when the story of the Iraqi 'super-gun' affair surfaced in the British press. In short, an unusually large cannon supposedly capable of firing battlefield nuclear shells over long distances

* Conservative MP for Thanet, Kent, for twenty-three years; government minister in charge of defence procurement under John Major's premiership in 1992–94; First Secretary to the Treasury in 1994–5. Convicted of perjury in 1999, for which he received an eighteen-month prison sentence.
† TV-am was the UK's first commercial breakfast-TV channel. Founded by the 'famous five' – David Frost, Michael Parkinson, Angela Rippon, Robert Kee, and Anna Ford, with Peter Jay as chief executive – TV-am was failing, which led to acrimonious resignations and a boardroom coup in which Peter Jay was replaced by Jonathan Aitken.

had been commissioned by Iraqi President Saddam Hussein and was manufactured by Sheffield Forgemasters, a UK-listed company on whose board another Aitken Hume director, Stuart Graham, sat. Gerald Bull, the inventor of the supergun had been assassinated – by Israeli Intelligence according to unsubstantiated rumours. Two investigating journalists had disappeared in mysterious circumstances. Stuart Graham was a former chief executive of Midland Bank, which was separately alleged to have provided a base for many years for a cell of British Intelligence agents. There was no obvious conclusion or connection to be drawn from these stories, but the fact that Wafic Saïd, Lee Ming Tee, and Stuart Graham were on the same (Aitken Hume) board sent the rumour mill into overdrive.

I had no special knowledge of any of this, nor ever came across anything untoward within the company, but its profile remained higher than was warranted by the size of our operations. Incidentally, in regard to the latter, it amused me that, as part of a rationalisation process, I sold our small unit-trust side to a youthful Martin Gilbert, thereby supplying his fledgling company, Aberdeen Asset Management, with their first 100 million pounds under management. The transaction received favourable substantive comment in the *Financial Times*. I seem to recall that I had arranged for one of our banks to advance some of the purchase price to Martin at that time. Unfortunately, Aberdeen did not remain a banking customer for long, continuing its climb to dizzy heights without us.

But I digress, I continued on at Aitken Hume after the failed coup, and I now sold Eaton Place and upgraded myself in acquiring a splendid new bachelor flat at 45 Eaton Square, also decorated by Sofia Stainton at a most reasonable cost. Sadly, my love affair with Valerie spluttered simultaneously to an end. We all know how difficult it is to sustain long-distance relationships at the best of times, but as I have intimated earlier, Valerie had come to believe the myth put about by her press agent that we were engaged to be married. When it became quite obvious that I was unable to sustain such a commitment, she understandably resumed her acting career in Los Angeles, angrily, but with her usual vigour. I am afraid she and many of her friends considered that I did not behave well, that I had abandoned a serious commitment. Such are the risks of believing one's own publicity. But there was nothing I could do. I had not been divorced long, I had my son, and at that time I had no intention of ever settling down again.

My fortieth birthday came and went. I took over Mark's Club and threw a dinner for seventy guests including Wafic and Jonathan with their wives. Wafic, with great generosity, gave me a superb set of diamond studs and cufflinks from Asprey. My friend Naim Attallah, the publisher of *By Victories Undone*, but simultaneously the then chief executive of Asprey, was another guest, and one uniquely qualified to value Wafic's present to me. Thus, through Naim I was able to return them in exchange for a substantial credit note. This became the source of many small but impressive presents from Asprey to girlfriends for many years, enhancing considerably my own reputation among the fairer sex at the time. I had good reason to be grateful to Wafic.

Some weeks later, in a lift in The Ritz, whilst departing early from a charity function, I literally bumped into Ira von Fürstenberg, whom I had not seen since before my marriage to Jan. I invited her for a nightcap to Annabel's where it took less than one dance for us to fall back into each other's arms as if time had stood still; it was the late 1970s again, and we were back in my little house in Godfrey Street. Ira had been having a serious relationship with the widowed Prince Rainier of Monaco for the previous two years. Many observers had assumed she would become the new First Lady of the Principality. It was not to be. Ira was a proud person and hardly mentioned it, but I felt she had been somewhat bruised by the experience.

Ira was as always a tremendous asset at my business dinners. She also accompanied me to the launch party of *By Victories Undone*, a fact much photographed and reported upon in the press at the time – as was the absence of Valerie and the end of that particular affair.*

The launch party was, appropriately enough, held at Aspinalls, the smartest casino in London. Attended by many friends, fellow gamblers, celebrities, and pretty girls, the party was covered extensively in both the *Daily Mail* and the *Daily Express*. It was all great fun and a terrific success, except for one low moment, courtesy of a man with whom I had previously been on perfectly friendly terms.

By coincidence, Roald Dahl happened to be playing blackjack upstairs that night at Aspinalls. In his capacity as publisher, Naim Attallah encouraged me to ask Roald to come down and join us for a glass of champagne. Naim knew it would be excellent publicity for my book if the press saw Roald at the launch. It would have cost Roald nothing, perhaps all of fifteen minutes away from the gaming tables. He flatly refused me on the spurious grounds that he had some sort of feud with Naim. His behaviour was disappointing.

Even Norman, when asked by Naim for a quote, described *Victories* as having a plot 'full of surprising twists and turns', the characters as 'dark and venal', and the book as a 'bestseller for intelligent readers'. In fact, the hardback did sell well in London, for some time at number three on the Harrods bestseller list, briefly reaching number one. Reviews from as diverse newspapers as the *Wall Street Journal* and the *Guernsey Evening Post* were generally good. The *Independent*, however, called on the 'authors to fold their hands before it was too late!' I suppose we did in the end.

Radio chat shows, especially BBC Oxford and Capital radio were also kind to us. But undoubtedly, our best moment was when Simon MacCorkindale and Susan George acquired an option over the film rights for their production company Amy International. This exciting

---

* Indeed, the press alighted upon our renewed relationship with some zeal. A photograph of us under the headline 'Manoli Takes the Princess to the Pictures', for example, appearing in the *Daily Express* a month or so later, when Ira and I attended a private viewing of some of Hans Heinrich Thyssen-Bornemisza – 'Heini's' –priceless collection of paintings.

development unfortunately backfired, because when Amy renewed the rights the following year, and spent at least 30,000 pounds on commissioning what turned out to be an awful screenplay, we were convinced the film would indeed be made. Also, Simon was keen to play Jamie, a role that could literally have been written for him. Accordingly, we delayed the sale of the paperback rights and a potential sequel, in the belief that a film would make these much more valuable. Sadly, Amy went out of business; the film was never made, and the paperback rights by then worth little.

In any case, for the next six months, Ira and I were happy and largely inseparable. But life's twists and turns can be full of irony. We were dining at the Hôtel du Palais in Biarritz – a glorious spot that had gone somewhat out of fashion of late, but one which Ira's frequent presence would restore to much of its former popularity in due course – when Ira became unexpectedly serious about our future together.

It was my turn to be surprised. I hadn't expected it. Nine years earlier, just before Ira had disappeared with the Swiss ski instructor, I would have given anything for this, but now … the timing was sadly wrong. It was too late. Too late for two reasons: I still had no intention of ever committing to marriage again, especially once more with a glamorous woman considerably wealthier and better known than me. And also, deep down, I knew that just as I had foolishly married Jan on the rebound from Ira, Ira was at that time herself on the rebound from Prince Rainier. I don't think she was herself. It would never have worked out for either of us.

I am still convinced I was right about that. Both Ira and I were each left in a deeply depressed state. Mine actually, I believe, much worse than hers. I was truly sad. Nevertheless, at Ira's volition, we parted for good this time. We did not see each other until a party at the media mogul Conrad Black's nearly ten years later, at which point I had finally just married again. We are now at least firm friends, but for many years I wondered how different our lives might have been had the sequence of events been reversed. Timing really is everything.

The timing wasn't particularly good, as it turned out, for a magazine article about me in the April 1988 edition of *Harpers & Queen*. For some reason, this was cryptically entitled at the time of publication 'Manoli me Tangere' by an editor with clearly classical aspirations. Whether an accurate Latin translation would be 'Manoli touch me' or 'surely don't touch me' is unclear, as is the relevance of either.

A respected magazine journalist, Olinda Adeane, had contacted me to ask if I was prepared to be interviewed for a lifestyle profile for the prestigious publication. *By Victories Undone*, which had been published a few months earlier, was selling well. This was an obvious opportunity to give it more coverage. I agreed to the interview on the following provisos: that I could mention the book, that I would be portrayed as a serious businessman in the context of the turnaround of Aitken Hume's fortunes, and that there would be no mention of any girlfriends or anything frivolous of that sort. I also asked for the right of approval of the final copy. I had the Aitken Hume shareholders and my board colleagues very much in mind.

Olinda checked with the editor, Nicholas Coleridge, and received definite assurances from him on all of these issues.

The interview went reasonably well. True to her word, Olinda wrote an amusing, balanced piece which I considered good promotional content for the book, though reading it today I think I was far too pleased with myself. It was also complimentary about my work at Aitken Hume. I was glad to approve it, and to submit a flattering photograph of myself to accompany the text.

That month's edition was published. I feverishly searched through the magazine in joyous anticipation, until I came upon the main section. My heart sank like an enormous stone – the section was headed 'Playboys'. The introductory paragraph by the editor postulated that the 'old fashioned, stylish playboy' of the 1920s and '30s was making a comeback. About fifty well-known social figures were then listed with no more than a short paragraph, or in most cases a couple of lines, on each person.

The first person directly described as an old-fashioned playboy, the only one with a full-length profile of two and a half pages, together with a quarter-page photograph, was me. I was horrified. I had been 'stitched up like a kipper', as my gambling friends would have said.

Not a word of the article I had approved had been changed, the flattering photograph I now hated continued to stare out at me. But the placement was everything. It was terrible publicity for me professionally (if actually not for the book). The editor must have known it. I telephoned Olinda in a fury, feeling totally betrayed. A playboy section of all things. And I was the lead article!

Olinda swore she too was shocked and had been manipulated by her editor. That she had been given no inkling of any of this when she innocently wrote her piece. She had been commissioned, after all. She was not a staff reporter ... she was not a party to overall content.

I believed Olinda, but Coleridge had behaved badly. Either way, the damage had been done. I no longer hold it against Nicholas, but this was a milestone in my learning curve of how ruthless and devious the press can be.

CHAPTER FOURTEEN

The 1990s: Enter Emily Todhunter

I HAD MET KEITH AND ANN BARISH IN NEW YORK; THEY WERE friends of Jan's. Keith in particular was an interesting character, although I was closer to Ann. As a young, attractive businessman, Keith had made his first fortune in his twenties through a controversial mutual fund company of principally Latin American investors. He moved to Los Angeles, where he set up a film-production company that found early success with large-budget films such as *Sophie's Choice* and *Ironweed*, both with Meryl Streep – the former bringing her a Best Actress Oscar. At this point, Keith had the inspiration that became the restaurant chain Planet Hollywood. Movie memorabilia-themed restaurants were opened in key cities around the United States and Western Europe in careful coordination, a gap of a year between each one. These openings were conducted with great fanfare, in the manner of a major film premiere. Keith had hit upon the brilliant idea of giving a couple of percentage points each to Arnold Schwarzenegger, Bruce Willis, and Sylvester Stallone in return for their attendance at every opening. This in turn brought several additional stars to the event, guaranteeing maximum local publicity. It was a highly effective marketing plan.

I was invited to the London opening at its location just off Piccadilly Circus. The lunchtime launch was a glittering affair. Ahead of me on the red carpet were many famous faces from the entertainment industry. They stood around, chatting in small groups, posing for the jostling

132

photographers. The photographers of course had no interest in me, and I threaded my way through the decorative throng to the relative peace of the lobby inside, where I gratefully accepted a glass of champagne. There was a real sense of occasion, a tangible buzz of excitement.

The celebrities drifted in, we started to find our seats for lunch. Ann showed me to her table, where I was seated between Melanie Griffiths and Demi Moore. The other men were Danny Glover and Patrick Swayze. I had met none of them before. A few yards away, Bruce Willis was crooning incomprehensibly into a stand-up microphone. Everyone was in a jolly mood, our table was animated and fun. Danny and Patrick were friendly and amusing, but I found Demi to be particularly charming company. She made a great effort with me, even laughing at my lame joke in reference to her latest film *Indecent Proposal* – I doubled the price and offered her two million dollars for one night – thereby revealing her formidable talent as an actress. By the end of lunch, we had bonded. Melanie Griffiths, on the other hand, was suffering from the effects of a seriously late night. She tried gamely to be entertaining, but her communication skills were somewhat suspended. Still, that did not dampen everyone's good spirits. I returned to the office in a glorious mood.

That evening, there was to be a celebratory dinner for the Hollywood insiders. Ann invited me, simultaneously asking if I could reserve two large tables at Harry's Bar, since I was the only member. It was the least I could do. Again, I had a terrific time, but left early since I had an early-morning meeting the next day. The meeting lasted into the afternoon, and I returned to my office to find that Mark Birley had called twice. I telephoned him immediately, slightly concerned, realising Mark must have something urgent on his mind. In fact, Mark was furious. The object of his anger was me. The reason apparently, when he was calm enough to explain, was that sometime after I left, Don Johnson and Melanie Griffiths had locked themselves into the ladies' at Harry's Bar for around forty minutes, denying access to other guests and members. Complaints had flooded in the next morning. I was to blame, because I had broken a cardinal rule of membership by leaving my guests, for whom I was responsible, alone in the club. Mark gave me a severe lecture. All members at all his clubs were circulated with a reiteration of this rule, which from then on was rigidly enforced – at least as far as I was concerned.

❧

My time at Aitken Hume was drawing to an inevitable close. On the one hand, the immediate task had been done with the restoration of profitability, on the other hand, Tony's prediction – that the controlling shareholders on the board would have no interest in any major acquisitions that would dilute their stake – was inescapable. In fact, the company was shrinking after I sold the life insurance subsidiary and its unit trust side. Moreover, Wafic Saïd had left the board to concentrate on his own affairs, nominating an aggressive, egotistical Syrian banker called Ziad Idilby to be his replacement. With Idilby, board meetings became increasingly uncongenial and acrimonious, any suggestions I had were now rudely dismissed out of hand. In 1990, I resigned on a matter of principle regarding the mooted sale of another subsidiary. This occasioned a long article by Jeff Randall, the new City editor of the *Sunday Times*, favourable to me, speculating on my reasons for leaving. Aitken Hume's PR advisor Tim Bell had promised me a fair ride in the press, but the board delayed settling their contractual liability to me and, in the meantime, the 'City Diary' of the *Daily Telegraph* – at Jonathan Aitken's instigation – described my departure as a 'flouncing out'. Intensely irritated, I instructed the specialist firm of Carter-Ruck to issue proceedings for defamation against the *Telegraph*. After the intervention of Tim Bell, this was settled in an elegant manner. As a result, the same column later quoted me as saying my resignation had been principled, whilst in addition mentioning my novel, Norman Mailer, and a new project I had devised with my brother Niki – Armchair Athletes. The *Telegraph* also paid my legal costs.

Armchair Athletes was an attempt to raise funds for those GB athletes taking part in minority sports in the 1992 winter and summer Olympic

Games that had insufficient funds through lack of government assistance or commercial sponsorship. In those days before the National Lottery, sport, in particular minority sports, were chronically underfunded. In the 1988 Summer Olympics in Seoul, for example, Great Britain had come twelfth in the overall medals table. Thanks largely to National Lottery funds, by comparison, in 2016 Great Britain had risen to third place and came second in gold medals alone. Armchair Athletes was an early attempt to achieve a modest improvement at that time. It was formed by my brother, as managing director, myself as chairman, and a close friend of ours, Alan Campbell. Alan was a contemporary of Niki's at university, and he owned a small but successful advertising boutique based in Convent Garden where he provided office space. A girlfriend, Carol Bennet, invested alongside us and provided sterling support as an associate director.

Armchair Athletes then framed an appeal to those identifying as 'couch potatoes' among the public to donate ten pounds each to raise one million pounds for a range of twelve sports, including fencing, rowing, boxing, swimming, skiing, bobsledding, and the luge. Under our slogan 'Let Britain Compete', Niki and I hosted a large launch party at the Lansdowne Club off Berkeley Square. This was extremely well attended by the national coaches and the leading athletes of the relevant sports. MPs Sir Robert Rhodes James, Simon Burns, and Tom Pendry came to support, as did Imran Khan and Colin Ingleby-Mackenzie, good friends of mine from the rather different world of cricket. Imran, in an act worthy of a future Prime Minister of Pakistan, opened the bowling with a pledge of 100 pounds as opposed to ten. The press gave us enthusiastic backing. Most of the country's regional newspapers covered the event, as did the leading sports correspondents of the *Times*, the *Sunday Times*, and the *Daily Mail*. The *Daily Express* gossip column seized the opportunity to remark upon my personal life, but at least promoted the cause. Even Mark Birley made a rare public appearance at the Lansdowne. We tried our best. However, despite this outburst of patriotic newspaper fervour and many months of hard work, only a few thousand pounds were raised.

Britain barely managed fourteenth place in the medals table in the 1992 Summer Olympics in Barcelona. How times have changed for the better.

A similarly marked change was taking place in my relationship with Jan. Her marriage to Minot Amory had already defused a certain amount of her bitterness towards me, the recent birth of her second son seemed to complete that process, and we were actually beginning to bond over the progress of John, who was now eleven years old.

It was always more dangerous to be on friendly rather than hostile terms with Jan, since the inevitable stiletto between the shoulder blades would sink deeper with one's guard down. I was to relearn this lesson in spades a couple of years later, but for the moment, I naïvely thought we had ended up decent friends as the parents of the child we shared.

Jan's social life also was beginning to coincide with mine again, and we both found ourselves attending a marvellous ball in Venice that year given by our mutual friend Count Giovanni Volpi at the magnificent Palazzo Volpi. Giovanni's father had inaugurated the Venice Film Festival there in the 1930s; Giovanni was to resuscitate this glamorous annual occasion soon afterwards, but this was the first Volpi Ball for many years. It was an exceptional experience – the Grand Canal ablaze with flaming torches along its length on either side, the elegant guests arriving at the Palazzo in lamp-lit gondolas, stepping on to the crimson-carpeted steps to be greeted by white-coated staff with endless silver trays laden with champagne and buckets of iced caviar. Within the grand Palazzo, its walls covered in priceless paintings, there were several bands playing in different staterooms as everyone danced through the night, stopping only to dine for breakfast off the huge buffet tables, and to replenish their drinks from the many attentive waiters.

Jan had come without her husband. True to form, the focus of her attention became Winston Churchill, the grandson of the great man. 'Young Winston' was a kind, genial, attractive man with a quirky, irrev-erent sense of humour. He had been a Conservative MP for several years until a recent decision to end his political career, and, as it turned out, his first marriage was also entering its final stages. Sensing this,

Jan flirted with him outrageously. Winston did seem to fall under her spell for a short time, but I mention this only to record that, as a result, I too met Winston that evening in Venice, and we became firm friends thereafter. We were to see quite a lot of each other in London over the next eighteen years, during which he managed to evade Jan's pursuit of him, ignore the torrent of newspaper publicity she brought down upon his head, and to marry the adorable Luce Danielson whom I liked very much. Tragically, Winston died of cancer at the relatively early age of sixty-nine in 2010. I always think of Winston with great affection, but my recollection of his memorial service at St. Margaret's, Westminster is a little more complicated.

On that day, I dutifully reported to the Porters' Lodge of St. Margaret's Church in the shadow of Westminster Abbey, naturally somewhat depressed. Luce had invited me, and I duly gave my name. A young porter carefully studied the list of guests. Asked again to spell my name, it was met with a puzzled frown, a shake of the head. My name apparently was nowhere to be found. Sadly, I shrugged, inwardly telling my old friend that I was sorry, but I had tried. I made to walk away.

'Just a moment, sir,' the older porter said in a kindly fashion. He reached towards several piles of coloured cards, giving me a green one. He pointed towards the church. I thanked him. As I turned to leave, clutching my card, I heard him say to his colleague with a sigh, 'It's a bloody awful job, poor sod, but someone's got to do it.'

I shrugged off this strange remark and made my way to the church's imposing entrance. There, I was met by one of the ushers, smartly dressed in a well-tailored tailcoat. It was the Duke of Marlborough, a cousin of Winston's. We knew each other reasonably well. Sunny Marlborough asked for my card but looked puzzled when I produced it. Now it was his turn to sigh as he beckoned me to follow him. The benches were colour-coded. My sense of unreality grew as we passed row after row of crowded benches on our way towards the green ones which were at the front of the large church. At the fourth row from the front, in the centre aisle, Sunny finally stopped at an empty bench. He gestured to me to take a seat on the aisle and stiffly walked away, somewhat disapprovingly. I sat alone for some minutes, feeling extremely awkward.

The rest of the church was packed; I was clearly in the wrong seat. The row in front of me began to fill. Nigel Lawson, Norman Lamont, Michael Heseltine, and other former Tory Cabinet Ministers filed in. There was a hush when Margaret Thatcher joined them at the end of their bench, immediately in front of me. More junior former ministers pushed passed me to join my row, coincidentally Jonathan Aitken among them. They all looked at me in surprise. Norman Lamont nodded to me in a friendly way – I had lately managed to enlist his support for a German property company I was advising – but that did not prevent him from commenting loudly that Michael Howard had a poor seat at the back. Winston's family were seated in the block to the left of ours, so that I was on the same level as many of them. His cousin, my old friend Nicholas Soames, glanced curiously at me. I felt embarrassed and fraudulent to be in such exalted company at such a lofty place of worship.

As the traditional service unfolded, its familiarity relaxed me. By the end, whilst the rows of guests began to file out in order after the family, I had recovered my equilibrium. As chance would have it, my turn to leave was immediately after Lady Thatcher's, so we slowly proceeded down the long aisle of the crowded church side by side. It may have been my imagination, but I was convinced I could hear a hum of interest from the great and the good as I passed with her. By the time I was close to the church door, I was in an exuberant mood, exulting in the reflected glory of our former Prime Minister whilst nodding gravely at the few people I knew at the back. I know Winston would have been highly amused, in fact I'm sure he metaphysically planned it. I never discovered why the porters gave me a green card, or what was meant by their remark, but on reflection I can only surmise they mistook me for an unknown junior Liberal minister in the new coalition government. It was, for me, a very special celebration of Winston's life.

❧

The 1990s marked an important new phase in my professional life. The venerable US partnership of Johnson & Higgins was the largest privately owned insurance broker in the world. It had arranged the insurance affairs of leading North American companies for nearly 200 years; its branch network serviced the needs of these now-multinational companies and encircled the globe. Eighty-five per cent of the Fortune 100 companies were their clients, sixty-five per cent of the Fortune 250. In London, a falling out with Willis Faber, the longstanding local partner, had led recently to the formation of a UK subsidiary. Johnson & Higgins Limited became overnight one of the most important Lloyd's insurance brokers. However, despite its large revenues, the UK operation was making net losses. The co-chairmen, Charles Carter and Nuno de Brito e Cunha, were highly talented brokers, well respected in the Lloyd's market. They had sold their own firm to Johnson & Higgins for a large sum, but they were instinctively more attracted to the continued expansion of the business than its rationalisation. They decided to appoint a professional managing director from outside the insurance industry for this purpose, and I was offered the job. The next six years were among the happiest of my career.

Soon after I started, two enormously joyful landmarks took place in my personal life. I met Emily Todhunter, the love of my life, to whom I would be married. And I managed to organise a place at Harrow School for my son, John, thereby smoothing the way for him to live in England. A particular blessing for me was the wonderfully close and uncomplicated relationship which sprang up instantly between him and Emily.

Emily was twenty-nine years old to my forty-four. From a solidly upper-middle-class English family, her looks are a wonderful mixture of English rose and Latin, the latter because of her dark hair and green eyes. This is enhanced by a smart-casual dress style which verges on the bohemian. Appropriately, I met Emily at a small dinner party given by Laurie Hunter and his second wife, Carlin, at their Chelsea house in Mallord Street. I remember as if it were yesterday, Emily perching on the arm of my chair to continue the conversation we had been having about her family's house in Ithaca, comparing that island to Kalymnos on the opposite side of Greece. She was already a well-known interior designer with many high-profile restaurants, nightclubs, and large country houses to her credit. Later, to these would be added super-yachts, skiing chalets, holiday homes, and grand city apartments.

I was immediately attracted to Emily but even stronger bonds were beginning to form. It was not long before we were spending a great deal of time together, both in London and Greece. However, as well as her looks and joie de vivre, Emily was obviously loyal, kind, and extremely decent; indeed, she really is a superior human being. This was beginning to push me in a direction I had thought to avoid for the remainder of my life. I had determined long ago that I did not want long-term commitment, another marriage, or more children. But there was nothing I could do. I loved her too much, and we knew we were meant for each other. For once in my life, the timing was perfect. I was lucky that she too was ready to settle down. Both our lives were approaching a completely new chapter.

Back at the office, I was initially alarmed that Charlie and Nuno had decided to leave Johnson & Higgins in a mission to raise newly designed corporate capital for the Lloyd's insurance market. The winds of change, driven by coinciding huge asbestos- and hurricane-related losses in the early 1990s, were sweeping through the underwriting syndicates, bankrupting many individual 'names' in the process. Capital was now in short supply, the very existence of the 400-year-old market hanging in the balance. Charlie and Nuno's initiative was bold, laudable even, but it was to take place under the stridently confident auspices of the American investment bank Salomon Brothers. My own experience of investment banking had taught me to beware bankers' overconfident forecasts for success in novel operations. I remembered many innovative financing ideas whose time had not quite arrived, no matter how successful they later became. Besides, I would miss my brothers-in-arms a great deal, we had become a successful, closely knit team. I pleaded in vain for them to stay, notwithstanding my imminent promotion by the US partners to chairman as well as managing director to fill the gap. Unfortunately, my scepticism was proved justified, Salomon had been far too optimistic. An insufficient amount of capital was raised for the underwriting syndicates from corporate sources. In time, this approach, together with the adoption of limited liability for individuals, was to save Lloyd's, but not just yet. Nevertheless, I was able to repay Charlie and Nuno's original faith in me by persuading our American owners to allow them to return as directors. This suited all of us, since they could continue to obtain new business in their own time without responsibilities for the running of the company, which they found irksome.

For the first time, both my private life and business life were stabilising simultaneously. Emily brought me luck. My cup was now overflowing. However, I had reckoned without Jan. This would prove a terrible mistake.

I should have realised much sooner that both my happiness with Emily, together with John's obvious enthusiasm for life in England and school at Harrow, would inevitably destroy any semblance of the friendship which I thought now existed between Jan and me. Jan's failed pursuit of Winston had contributed greatly to the failure of her fourth marriage. The publicity had helped her lose custody of her second son. Her jealousy of my happy situation, hidden at first, was to erupt with devastating consequences for everyone.

For some time I continued in blissful ignorance. I went to New York on business, taking Emily with me. Jan, all sweetness and light, gave a dinner for us at Elaine's restaurant. Many mutual friends were there, including the Mailers. I thought it was mere unfortunate coincidence that Valerie – dressed in a red leather trouser suit – was there dining with a girlfriend, watching balefully from a nearby table. This made Jan's (primarily male homosexual) guests uncomfortable and cast a pall over the evening. Norris Mailer, next to me, was convinced that Valerie's presence had been orchestrated, but I thought her overly dramatic. In hindsight, I realised she was right, and that the preponderance of male homosexuals was designed to discomfort Norman, who somewhat unfairly had the reputation of being homophobic.

⌒

A short and final digression about Norman Mailer. Much has been written about Norman's views and character, and certainly we didn't agree on everything, but he was extremely charismatic, and more affectionate in his own way than most ever realised. Equally, although Norman cultivated a macho image, in the way of his hero Ernest Hemingway, he loved women to an extreme – after all, he was married six times. I would like to recount a little about an evening we shared shortly before his death.

It must have been around 2005 that I last saw my dear friend. Norman had come over to London with Norris as guests of the Orange Book Awards for the annual presentation of their prestigious prize for women's fiction. At his request, Emily and I had received an invitation, but since our twin baby boys were slightly unwell, I went alone. It was an interesting occasion followed by a dinner at which I was placed on Norman and Norris' table, along with Germaine Greer, the writer Josephine Hart, and her husband, Maurice Saatchi. It happened that I had met the Saatchis a couple of times recently at the home of my friends Nicholas and Serena Soames, so I was able to introduce Josephine to Norris, knowing they were kindred spirits and would get on well, which they did.

I was seated between an extremely pretty, if slightly vacuous, female TV presenter, whose name I cannot recall, and a rather intense Germaine Greer. The girls did not hit it off, despite the obvious hero worship which the presenter showed to Germaine Greer – perhaps because of it. I did my best to keep the peace, cracking a few silly jokes occasionally, but I don't think this helped too much. Nevertheless, I enjoyed myself immensely, still managing to have entertaining conversations on either side.

It was an amusing evening in many ways. Norman was looking frail for the first time, but was in particularly good form, enjoying his ironic guest-of-honour status at an event with distinct feminist undertones. He went back some way with Germaine Greer; their paths crossed many times. For example, in the 1970s he had debated against four feminists including her, in a cult documentary film called *Town Bloody Hall* in which, by general consent, she had bested him, but I think they were basically always on good terms.

Towards the end of dinner, Norman leaned down the table in her direction.

'Germaine, you look worried,' he called, 'is everything alright? Is Manoli being nice to you?'

'I'm fine, Norman,' came a cutting reply. 'If you must know, I was worrying about finances. In case you hadn't noticed, none of us is getting any younger!'

'Ah, no need to worry,' Norman sat up straight, his face beaming. 'How much do you need? I can show you exactly how to raise one, maybe two, million dollars for your pension right now. It'll only take you a few minutes.'

'Okay, Norman. Tell me then …,' she sighed, correctly anticipating some ridiculous idea.

'We just need to call over one of those photographers to take pictures of you and me, right now … Just the two of us …. Only you have to be giving me a blowjob!' Norman said with a flourish. 'Then we syndicate them worldwide!'

He burst out laughing, as did I. And, to be fair, although she wasn't expecting quite that, a smile began to dispel the severity of the look on Germaine's face, swiftly followed by a guffaw. 'Oh, Norman.' She said resignedly, shaking her head.

This then allowed everyone else to laugh uproariously. Once a trouper …

The evening drew to a close. Norris kissed me goodnight, but Norman hugged me tightly. He lowered his head, pointing at his forehead. With great tenderness we butted them together gently, as always, but this time hardly touching. Norman died two years later in America. I would never see him again, and I think he knew it.

❧

I had best return to my increasingly strained relations with Jan. I'd dismissed the incident at Elaine's and others as examples of Jan's gratuitously nasty nature after one drink too many. A lot harder to shake off were reports that were filtering back of her telephoning my senior partners in New York late at night to make vitriolic comments about me. It says a great deal about the character of those partners that they refused to take Jan's ramblings seriously and did not hold her behaviour against me. In fact, on the contrary. The UK operation was growing in leaps and bounds, profits were soaring; I had moved us to spanking new, refurbished offices in Aldgate in the heart of the insurance district, the opening attended by Ted Heath who made a welcoming speech; we were now an important and influential Lloyd's broker. In 1994, we won the Queen's Award for Exports, to the delight of the Americans, and I was invited to a reception hosted by the Queen at Buckingham Palace. With the exception of the Prince of Wales who was abroad, all the senior royals were present, really working the room, as they say in America. I was impressed by their diligence and particularly by the instant bonhomie of Prince Philip towards me when he read my name card. 'I'm Greek too, you know!' he said. 'Yes, Sir. I did realise,' I replied gravely. He beckoned me back over when the receiving line broke up, and we each had a large scotch together. He was delightfully welcoming and amusing.

A few months later, Emily and I visited Gstaad where John was spending a few days over New Year skiing with his mother. Jan's behaviour towards us was increasingly bizarre in public, designed to embarrass. She shouted aggressively at Emily in the Palace Hotel on New Year's Eve, upset at having mislaid the cloakroom ticket for her lynx coat, which she announced to a crowded lobby had been a parting present from Stavros Niarchos.

Nevertheless, the months sped by. I visited Emily at her parents' house in Ithaca, she came to stay with me in Kalymnos. I got on well with her family, and my father adored her, as did Niki. To John she had already become a wise and affectionate stepmother. In July of 1995 we became engaged, the wedding to take place in December. We should have married immediately.

CHAPTER FIFTEEN

Scandal

THE BRITISH PRESS COVERED OUR ENGAGEMENT WITH GREAT interest, 'On Her Tod No More' ran the headline in Nigel Dempster's piece in the *Daily Mail*; 'Happy Ending' ran Ross Benson's tagline in the *Daily Express*. Both mentioned Johnson & Higgins and Emily's interior design business, together with Jan and a couple of early respective girlfriends and boyfriends. In my case, these were principally Ira and Valerie, so I found it slightly curious that the *Express* also mentioned that I had 'escorted' a little-known actress who had appeared in a James Bond film for no more than two minutes. It was true that I had met this girl – actually a woman of forty-two years old with three teenage daughters – over a year before, and that a mild dalliance had taken place at that time, but we had hardly 'been out', and so couldn't have been seen out to dinner together. There had been no reason to hide what was simply a minor moment. However, I knew that the actress was friendly with Benson, assumed he was giving her a little free publicity, and thought no more about it. I also had no reason to believe she and I were not on decent terms.

Imagine, therefore, my shock when this actress (whom I will not dignify by naming) then telephoned me out of the blue to inform me in a staged, husky voice that she was pregnant and that I was the father. My first reaction was to burst out laughing. I really did think this must be a joke, which annoyed her intensely. Once I realised this was not a joke, I told her to stop being ridiculous and hung-up. I was not at all worried, since if she really was pregnant it could not possibly have anything to do with me, but I felt I should tell Emily about the call, which was not going to be particularly welcome news – although I was confident Emily would be as undisturbed as she turned out to be. On the other hand, I did become slightly concerned when I heard a few days later that the actress was trying to get her story printed in the newspapers. But again, I was not actually worried since I did not believe any newspaper would dare to print such manifest rubbish. As the clock ticked down towards December, all went quiet. It seemed to have been a non-event. But, as a precaution, I retained a private detective through my brother to try to discover what was behind this ludicrous allegation.

Emily and I were busy making preparations for our wedding to take place at the local village church where her father, Michael Todhunter, was the churchwarden. Emily had attended this church since childhood. This was important to her father, I was happy to agree, and I arranged for two Greek Orthodox Bishops to come down from London to administer a short ten-minute blessing after the service. Michael Todhunter, was not thrilled about it, but the guests would just have to wait another ten minutes. I asked John, now fourteen, to be my best man. The date was set for Friday the 1st of December.

Jan called, ostensibly to talk about John, but actually to discover the wedding arrangements. I was surprised that she assumed she would be invited to the ceremony and unprepared for her anger when I told her how inappropriate this would be. She insisted that we were friends now, that since John would be my best man, this would be perfectly normal. She told me how hurt she was to be excluded before she hung up. This extreme reaction puzzled me. Sometime later, the private detective reported back. Through a contact at British Telecom, he had obtained a copy of the actress's quarterly telephone bill. Horrified, in shock, I could hardly believe my eyes – every day for the last several weeks multiple telephone calls had been made by her to Jan, and returned to her from Jan.

It dawned on me that this could now become a major problem. I still couldn't quite believe the newspapers would print anything libellous without proof, but I knew only too well the diabolical energy Jan could summon up to support a campaign of lies and innuendo.

Three days before the wedding, during the afternoon of Tuesday the 28th of November, my worst fears were realised. Jeff Randall, the City Editor of the *Sunday Times*, telephoned to warn me of rumours that both the *Mail* and the *Express* were planning to run the actress's fantasy story the following morning. It was clear to me that Jan had intervened to persuade the columnists that she could corroborate the story, that it was true, that they should publish it. Jan was giving the actress the credibility she lacked. Aghast, I called Nigel Dempster who told me there was nothing he could do; he had to cover the story because Ross Benson was going to anyway. Benson said the same about Dempster. I was caught between rival gossip columnists. Jeff, a friend, advised me that only Tim Bell was sufficiently influential with the editors of both newspapers to get the articles spiked, but it was early evening by now and I couldn't reach Tim anywhere. I called Barbara Amiel, a close former girlfriend now married to Conrad Black, the owner of the *Daily Telegraph*. Barbara tried to help by calling Lady Stevens whose husband owned the *Express*, but she had gone to dinner. I was on my own. At least Emily was a tower of strength. She was the only important consideration for me. I knew the story would damage my career whatever happened. Jan had been trying to accomplish that ever since Emily and I became engaged. I knew Emily well enough to know she would dismiss it out of hand, but I was concerned that this would be embarrassing for her family and their friends, which was bound to upset her. In the final analysis, her family took it very well, but I'm sure they must have put on brave faces from time to time. My last throw of the dice was to have my brother's law firm issue formal letters to both newspaper columnists, warning that they published at their peril. I did not expect them to have much effect.

The lead articles of the Diary pages of both the *Mail* and *Express* the following day were on the story in all its excruciatingly mythical detail. They included pictures of the actress, as well as mine and Emily's engagement photographs taken in July. The *Mail*'s headline was that the actress 'Stars in Greek tragedy', the *Express* had 'Shadow Cast over Society Wedding'. They could not have been worse write-ups, containing extensive quotes from her to the effect that she was seventeen weeks pregnant, a result of a passionate romance with me, that the baby was a girl. My strenuous denials were included, as were quotes from Emily expressing her disgust at the woman's behaviour. Yet, although the actress's claims came across as unstable ravings, the damage had been done.

The day before the wedding passed in a blur. The actress, no doubt still under Jan's tutelage, followed up with interviews with other journalists, in the *Mail* and *Express*, whilst failing to interest the *News of the World*. However, after the broadside of the previous day, a more cautious tone was being adopted in these articles. Further, in an early sign of scepticism, under the headline 'You must be kidding', Nigel Dempster now wrote that the claims made by the actress 'could end up in the libel court'. He quoted a close friend of hers as saying 'I'll believe it when she has it'. In addition, the actress said, 'Don't ask me for proof I'm having a baby – it would be too demeaning', which spoke volumes since she could not legally be compelled to prove anything at this stage. The only unavoidable proof would come after any baby was born.

The day of the wedding was an extremely happy one. The village church in Berkshire was bedecked with lovely flowers, packed with friends. A delicious, jolly lunch followed at Emily's parents' house, a classic Georgian rectory which had been the home of John Betjeman for many years. Emily's mother, Caroline Todhunter, had lovingly cultivated a fabulous garden there over decades which was occasionally open to the public, and despite the frost it provided a glorious background bathed in winter sunshine. During the church service, there was some concern among guests that the actress might make a dramatic appearance, but my brother was in touch with the private detective. He was following her and reported her to be in Hampstead at the time. The press who turned up outside the church in the hope of witnessing some sort of scene were disappointed. They were restricted to reporting only that our wedding had taken place.

I had rented for weekends a converted barn in the picturesque Cotswold village of Sapperton from the Bathurst Estate, and on the Sunday after the wedding we gave a lunch party for 150 of our mainly London friends. This too was a great success, photographed and covered in *Tatler* magazine. Taki Theodoracopoulos, for the 'Atticus' column of the *Sunday Times* that morning, ran a supportive item, 'Laughable Wedding Present', suggesting that 'there is nothing better than laughing at a woman scorned'. I did not know Taki well, he had been much closer to Emily, but I had always liked him. Certainly, when other journalists were cruel, he went out of his way to be kind. I will always remember this.

It had been an exhausting, but in a strange way exhilarating, introduction to married life for both of us. The past few days had precisely the opposite effect intended by Jan and her little marionette. Emily and I had bonded even more closely in the face of the onslaught. Nearly twenty-five years later, I am convinced this was part of the original glue that has helped to keep us so happy.

It was not a surprise that early in the New Year, the *Express* reported that the actress claimed she had been mugged in Kensington with the loss of cash and her mobile phone. It was even less of a surprise that the *Mail* and *Express* carried stories in February of a subsequent miscarriage. In the *Mail*, the actress was quoted as having told friends the 'foetus was buried in a field in the country'. The evidence had conveniently disappeared. Furthermore, the *Mail's* Diary column stated that the police had no record of any mugging incident so far that year in the Kensington, Chelsea, or Fulham areas involving a woman by this name. Finally, for the first time publicly making the link, its readers were told that Jan was arriving in London 'to commiserate with' the actress.

The disgusting sham had run its course, the tissue of lies exposed. The question was, what should I do about it? Galling though it was, there was no point suing the actress. She had no money from which to recover damages, she wouldn't even be able to pay my costs. Jan had played too hidden a role to be legally vulnerable. Turning to the newspapers, the *Mail* had joined my side after Dempster had shared in breaking the story and then perceived I would be vindicated. That left the *Express*. Emily persuaded me that we should move on with our lives, putting this awful time behind us. I agreed that it didn't make sense to embark upon lengthy, expensive, litigation, but I did ask Barbara Black if she could set up a meeting with Lord Stevens, the proprietor. This she did.

A tailcoated butler met me at eleven that morning at the entrance to the top floor of the Express Newspapers building on Hammersmith Bridge. These were the chairman's private offices. I followed him down a long, ornate, dark corridor, past marble busts of the Lords Beaverbrook and Stevens. The butler showed me silently into a dining room where at the end of a long table, perched on top of a large pile of cushions, the small figure of Lord Stevens was seated. He waved me to a dining chair where I sat and accepted a bone-china cup of coffee on a silver tray, poured from a silver pot by a different but equally attentive butler. This man with the pale face and white hair, I reminded myself, had been Robert Maxwell's partner.

'Now then,' Stevens said breezily, 'how can I help?'

Ignoring the question, I launched into a condemnation of his paper's involvement in the libellous nonsense about me. It was obvious he knew the facts well.

He frowned, leaning over to one side of his end of the table. He pretended to consult a memorandum.

Stevens appeared to ponder for a moment, 'I see that our information is that the foetus is buried in a field. Nothing therefore can be proven.'

He smiled triumphantly in an irritating manner.

'Interesting, Lord Stevens,' I was prepared for this, 'because if you believe that pack of lies, you must also believe that the foetus was disposed of illegally without a death certificate, that it was over six months old and therefore, if you really do have firm information, you are an accessory to murder.'

If it were possible, Stevens' face paled a little more. He sat back on his cushions.

'These reporters can be so irresponsible,' he sighed theatrically. 'What do you want?'

'An apology, damages, and my legal costs,' I replied.

'A 10,000-pound payment towards legal costs, no specific apology, but a nice article about you and your wife. All to be described as an amicable settlement,' he countered.

I agreed. I didn't care about the money. My legal fees were negligible anyway. I knew the only way to get an open apology from almost any newspaper was to win a lengthy lawsuit. Emily was right, we had to move on now, put this episode behind us. We had our vindication; to pursue revenge would be corrosive negative energy. Besides, we now had the fantastic news that Emily was pregnant. A 'nice article' duly appeared in the *Express* with a flattering synopsis of Emily's recent projects, an assertion that Emily's pregnancy was 'proof of [our] triumph over allegations made at the time of [our] wedding', with a quote from me as to how hurtful the nonsensical allegations had been. It ended with the newspaper wishing us well. The *Mail* followed suit, adding that John was going to be our child's godfather.

We began to relax, to look forward to our life together, to the birth of our child. The storm had passed, it was all over now – or so we thought.

Jan's campaign against us was not quite over, but she was forced to come into the open now. Under a headline 'Just Charge it to My Ex, says Jan', the *Mail* printed an article describing a dinner she gave for the actress and others at Mimmo's restaurant, at which I had an account, and where there were two photographs of me kindly placed by my friend Mimmo on the wall.* No doubt this restaurant had been chosen to cause me maximum embarrassment. Large quantities of champagne

---

* I was honoured to be included on Mimmo's legendary walls. This randomly taken collection of photographs, depicting celebrities from film, TV, and sport, with the proprietor often in shot with his arm around them, evolved into an extraordinary gallery over the years.

and caviar were consumed, but when presented with the bill, Jan left without paying, giving instructions to send it to me. I refused of course; after an ensuing spat, Jan sent a cheque round to Mimmo's to settle the bill. The final article was later that summer, again in the *Mail*, this time headed 'Exes to Grind about Manoli'. Described as being in an 'unholy alliance' together, it recounted how the actress, together with her three children, were currently staying with Jan in Newport. Of use to Jan no longer, the actress was cast aside by her soon afterwards.

A few unpleasant events continued. Emily found herself cancelled off flights upon reaching airports, her parents received anonymous phone calls falsely informing them their daughter was injured in a car crash in Florida, and a quite amusing incident occurred in our small local church in Sapperton on Christmas morning. During his sermon, the vicar thanked me for my great generosity. After the service I wished him a merry Christmas and asked him what he meant.

'Oh no!' he looked down in mortification and embarrassment, 'I should have known it was too good to be true. I should have known that a telephone call at two in the morning. ... I don't suppose your secretary did call ... no ... of course not. How stupid of me.' He shook his head sadly, 'So, no cash for the bell tower then? I thought so.' His voice tailed away as I apologetically explained that I was not able to underwrite the required amount of 50,000 pounds, despite the caller's assurance.

In January 1997, the final word in this sordid saga was written in the *Mail* on the joyful occasion of our daughter Olympia's birth. The birth was the subject of the item, and the last time a passing reference to the actress's libel was made in the national press. This wonderful event ended it. It was over. Jan had finally shot her bolt. I was never to speak to her again.

CHAPTER SIXTEEN

The End is Near

W ITH THE SALE OF JOHNSON & HIGGINS FOR TWO BILLION
dollars to Marsh & McLennan later that year, my career changed
direction again. I became executive chairman of a tiny AIM-listed company called Pacific Media plc, the only assets of which were a majority
stake in a cinema in Thailand, one in Singapore, and a minority interest
in an experimental Chinese-language broadcasting station in the UK.
There was hardly any cash in the bank, insolvency was looming.

The CEO and largest shareholder of Pacific Media was an Eton-
educated Malaysian from a wealthy family. His name was Clive Ng.
Clive, together with his partner Chi Chen, owned forty per cent of a
fledgling e-commerce operation called Asia Commerce.com. They made
a great team: Clive the consummate marketer, Chi the highly numerate
Singaporean, an engineer by training.

It seems incredible given the internet's ubiquity now, but 1997 was still
pioneering days for the World Wide Web everywhere. China then was a
market recognised for its enormous potential in general, but even further
behind the West in internet development and marketing. Clive and Chi
managed to sign exclusive internet joint-venture agreements between
leading American e-commerce companies and Asia Commerce.com to
develop Chinese capability. The dot-com boom was beginning, and Asia
Commerce was swept up in the madness. Clive and Chi had decided
to follow other initiatives by floating their company on the New York

Stock Exchange. They were besieged by brokers and investment banks desperate to be involved; Goldman Sachs valued Asia Commerce at one billion dollars before it even began trading; Clive and Chi's stake was correspondingly worth 400 million dollars.

It was my plan to persuade them to inject this stake into Pacific Media, to give Clive and Chi control, and turn it into their own public vehicle. I promised that within eighteen months, I would take Pacific Media up to a full London Stock Exchange listing. This would make its paper infinitely more acceptable, giving them the ability to expand quickly through acquisitions. They bought into the concept, Chi joining our board as CEO. I then negotiated the injection of their Asia Commerce stake. This was extremely market-sensitive information. Pacific Media shares were trading at 0.5 pence per share when I became chairman; after this transaction was completed, no more than six months later, they reached seven pence. During the following year, they were to reach a high of seventeen pence. The market capitalisation of the company thus increased from less than five million pounds to 300 million pounds in that same period. Although the dot-com mania produced several such stories, this spectacular increase in value made us the darlings of the small shareholder.

Further enjoyment was found in this venture due to two Wimbledon debentures acquired by the previous management of Pacific Media. By way of a coupon, and instead of cash, these paid out an annual total of eight seats at Centre Court throughout the Wimbledon fortnight, as well as the use of the comfortable debenture holders' lounge for food and drinks. These tickets were the ultimate in corporate hospitality. Whilst I used them mainly for the Wimbledon Men's Quarter- and Semi-finals from 1999 to 2004, my colleagues used them too.

One Semi-Final remains firmly fixed in my memory, but not because of the tennis.

I had invited my old friend Raymond Lewis, and the two of us went alone. We arrived an hour early, had a quick lunch in the lounge, and took our seats a few minutes before play was to begin. It was at this point that Raymond – who normally never recognised anyone – unfortunately spotted Jack Nicholson in the row in front. Without a word to me, he leaped up like a maniac and pushed his way over. Tapping a startled Nicholson on the shoulder, Raymond thrust his Order of Play under the actor's nose, demanding an autograph 'for his daughter'. To my intense embarrassment, Nicholson, who knew me a little, glanced at me and lifted his eyes to the sky.

'Okay,' he said exasperated, 'quickly, give me a pen.'

Raymond patted all his pockets. 'I don't have a pen. Don't you have a pen?' he raised his voice aggressively.

'No, I don't have a pen.' Nicholson's voice was soft but menacing.

'Don't you have a pen?' Raymond shouted at Nicholson's neighbour. I almost died. It was Paul McCartney. Luckily, Raymond didn't recognise him.

'I'm afraid I don't carry them,' Paul McCartney said with commendable equanimity.

The players were out on court now and warming up.

'Tell you what,' Nicholson drawled in that familiar tone, 'let's do this again. Later … much later!'

Raymond returned to his seat. Completely unabashed and not the slightest embarrassed. After the first set ended, Nicholson and McCartney abandoned their seats, only to resurface far out of reach on the other side of the court.

Aside from this slight embarrassment, Pacific Media began to assume cult status among small shareholders as probably the hottest penny stock on the market. It became a favourite of much of the financial press; the publicity that surrounded us on a daily basis was astonishing. Every time we announced a new partnership for Asia Commerce, our share price rocketed, making waves in all the national newspapers. I regularly appeared on Bloomberg television interviews. On the ridiculous side, the company was often rated top in a rather silly weekly financial quiz show on ITV called *Show Me the Money*. Our list of shareholders swelled to 43,000, on a par in sheer number terms with BP. I was continually asked in restaurants by barmen and waiters of my acquaintance whether they should buy more shares, even on occasion stopped in the street, and when we held general meetings of shareholders we had to hire Queen Elizabeth Hall to accommodate the numbers. Aware that without a solid, wholly owned business, Pacific Media's future would be uncertain when the e-commerce bubble burst, I raised seventy-five million pounds in a rights issue through my brother-in-law, an investment banker at Salomon Brothers. This we used to acquire TV Media, the largest TV shopping channel in Asia, and on the back of this we obtained a full listing on the London Stock Exchange. All this received prominent coverage in all the financial press.

In the midst of the excitement, however, there was an unpleasant moment. The *Daily Mirror* had been inspired by the dot-com boom to start a share-tipster column that followed penny shares. This was aptly named the 'City Slickers' column. I received several calls many times from James Hipwell, a journalist from this column. I never met him, and he was always courteous, but I had to be extremely circumspect with such people since their aim was always to ferret out price-sensitive information. Even when they received none, they would sometimes try to quote you out of context as part of their stock-buying tips the next day. I tried to avoid most of these calls. Hipwell and a colleague were ultimately jailed on insider-dealing charges, and although Pacific Media was not one of the stocks involved, I was summoned to give evidence against him by outlining the nature of his calls. I have to say that I found this a most depressing exercise. Hipwell seemed to me to be more naïve than anything else, and while he may have been guilty, I understood the amounts involved to be very small. Seeing him for the first time caged in the glass dock of Southwark Crown Court, I did feel sorry for him. I have met many people during my career who made large fortunes in this way. The great majority escaped scot-free because they were clever, sophisticated, and hard to prosecute.

I'm reminded of another occasion around the same time that I was in court, although this time someone far more famous than me was standing in the witness box. Desmond de Silva QC was one of my closest friends for over forty years. An imposing, tall, flamboyant figure, he was a brilliant criminal barrister with an incredibly sharp mind, great wit, and a flair for oratory in court, which I often thought owed much to the performance of Charles Laughton in *Witness for the Prosecution*.*

During the 1970s and '80s, Desmond was given the nickname 'The Scarlet Pimpernel' by the British press because of his extensive successes in representing British subjects in far-flung Commonwealth outposts that were accused of capital crimes and thus faced the death penalty, which still existed in many such countries. He almost always brought them home safely to Britain. Although he was nominally briefed by the Foreign Office, since the theoretical offences committed somehow involved spying, or something similar, I always believed that his real client was MI6.

Desmond's knighthood a few years ago was a result of his successful prosecution of Charles Taylor – the former President of Liberia – for war crimes, the first such indictment since the Nuremberg trials of Nazi war criminals in 1945–46. However, along the way, he represented many celebrities and sports stars. The latter was a practice built up after his defence of Bruce Grobbelaar and then others on match-fixing charges, his defence of John Terry, the Chelsea captain, regarding a nightclub fracas, and of managers Harry Redknapp and Ron Atkinson in connection with transfer allegations. Desmond became football's favourite barrister.

Desmond was in this incarnation when one day in the mid-1990s I had come to wait for him to finish in court. I was quite taken aback when the opposing counsel called a certain Mr. Reg Dwight to give evidence, and Elton John entered the witness stand. I cannot remember, if I ever knew, the cause of the trial, nor the nature of Elton John's evidence, although I assume he was testifying in his capacity as chairman of Watford Football Club, but I certainly remember the opening exchanges. Desmond once

---

* I highly recommend Desmond's book: Desmond de Silva, *Madam, Where are your Mangoes?* London: Quartet Books, 2017.

again conjured up the ghost of Charles Laughton in his pretence (I think), to the amusement of the jury, that he did not recognise Elton John and did not realise that 'Reg Dwight' was Elton John's real name.*

'Please tell the Court,' Desmond declaimed in patrician tones, 'what it is you do for a living, Mr. Dwight.'

'I'm a musician,' came the polite reply. Elton John smiled at the jury, most of whom were having difficulty keeping a straight face.

'Really, a musician, Mr. Dwight,' Desmond continued smoothly, 'and what instrument do you play?'

'Well, I play the piano … and I sing a bit,' Elton John replied as many of the jury began to giggle.

'Ah,' said Desmond, 'you sing. And do you make any money out of it?'

'It keeps the wolf from the door.' Elton John looked at the floor modestly.

'Goodness me, really, Mr. Dwight,' Desmond observed with a flourish, 'and so you frighten the wolf away by singing at it. You can't be very good!'

Elton John found this remark as funny as everyone else. I'm still not sure whether Desmond really recognised him or not.

I remained with Pacific Media until it was acquired by a rich Taiwanese family in 2004, and in the meantime my life with Emily was reaching milestone after milestone.

I had sold Eaton Square and, after the birth of my daughter Olympia, Emily and I moved to a uniquely cosy, small town house set in a little garden with a merrily splashing fountain hidden behind large walls at the Knightsbridge end of the Fulham Road. Harry Potter style, our address was 137½, Fulham Road. We kept the barn at Sapperton where we spent

* Sir Elton Hercules John was born Reginald Kenneth Dwight. Apparently, he named himself after Blues legends Elton Dean and Long John Baldry and the Roman god of hitting things.

many happy weekends, our closest friends as house guests. A frequent one was my dear friend, the late Jeremy Lloyd, best known as the author of *Are You Being Served?*, *'Allo, 'Allo!*, and *Captain Beaky*. Jeremy was one of the wittiest, most amusing men I have ever met. We were friends for forty years, and he adored both Emily and Olympia. I had one of the saddest tasks of my life when I was asked by his dear, adorable wife Lizzy to make speeches at both Jeremy's funeral and memorial services.*

I recall an amusing incident which I recounted at the memorial service and which was carried in the *Times* the next day. Emily and I were once staying with Jeremy and Lizzy at La Colombe d'Or Hotel in the South of France for Jeremy's birthday. Roger Moore, a close friend of Jeremy's, was staying too. One morning, I came downstairs to the lobby to find a large crowd of Japanese tourists. They were transfixed by the scene before them. Jeremy had mischievously asked Roger Moore to teach him to pronounce the line 'the name's Bond, James Bond'. Roger kept saying the line perfectly, with a straight face. Jeremy would repeat it with deliberately terrible timing. This went on and on. The onlookers were mystified, but in awe of the 'real James Bond'. They murmured excitedly to one another until finally Jeremy shouted 'James Bond' with a Japanese accent. After a moment of deep disappointment, the crowd melted silently away, completely confused – surely Bond was not Japanese …

The milestones continued with the enormous joy of Emily giving birth to identical twin boys, Mikey and Aleko, in 2002; John moved back to

---

* I spoke about my dear friend at both his funeral and memorial services; Charlotte Rampling gave a reading and Nigel Havers read a poem at the funeral; and Joanna Lumley, like me, attended both – she'd been married to Jeremy for a brief period. At the memorial, rock guitarist Jeff Beck played 'Somewhere over the Rainbow' on electric guitar (in E minor, I think). Beautiful, mournful, and cathartic, there was not a dry eye anywhere in the church. While he was playing, apparently, Beck was also praying that the E-string on his guitar wouldn't break from the strain; and no doubt, like me, he recalled Jeremy's debut as a percussionist playing a single 'ting' on the triangle onstage at one of his gigs. Lord Grade and the composer Leslie Bricusse spoke too. Vicki Michelle and Guy Siner attended to represent the cast of *'Allo, 'Allo'*. Bill Wyman and the late Terry O'Neill were also there.

work in the United States soon after graduating from University College London, my alma mater, soon afterwards; and Emily and I decided to move to the country to bring up the children. I had initial concerns, but it was unquestionably the right decision. We have a wonderful life in our modest, but comfortable Queen Anne farmhouse in Wiltshire, with our two Labradors, three ponies, two chickens, three cats, and a dozen white doves. We kept a modest sized flat in Knightsbridge into which we all crowd when necessary. And we have our house in Greece, on the island of Kalymnos, which all the children love. All homes decorated at very reasonable prices by Emily Todhunter .... And John, now married to the fantastic Liza and with two small daughters, joins us in Kalymnos every summer and in Wiltshire every Christmas.

Epilogue

DEAR READER, IF YOU ARE WITH ME STILL, I TAKE MY HAT OFF to you.

Solon, the wise lawgiver of ancient Athens, once said 'let no man claim he is happy until he is dead'. I am not yet dead, but I do claim to be extremely happy. For my own health, I do not much care. In any event, I like to think that I am well past the average life expectancy of those in ancient Athens in the sixth century BC. But for the health and happiness of Emily, my children, my granddaughters, my younger brother, his wife, and their daughter, I care very much indeed. I pray God continues to protect them all, and that the span of all their lives follows the natural state of things. I could not bear it otherwise. For the rest, the last twenty-five years have been the happiest of my life.

As I write, Emily has found great fulfilment and success in her work and our children. She is an amazing mother to them and a wonderful soulmate to me; John and Liza have two fabulous little girls, Anastasia and Eleanor; Olympia is close to graduation from Edinburgh University, having inherited her mother's artistic talents; and both Mikey and Aleko are doing well in their last year at Eton. I am proud of them all.

So there you have it. A life not particularly remarkable in its achievements. No blue plaque outside 45 Eaton Square alongside those of Metternich and Chamberlain. A business empire never built, a great philanthropic foundation never founded, nor a classic work of fiction for posterity written. Such talents as I had were far more modest. But they have brought me a sufficient amount of success with enough self-esteem to avoid many regrets, together with the ability to have fun, to laugh, to make and keep hold of good friends, and to enjoy the material benefits of this world to the absolute full.

I hope I do not tempt Fate when I say that for everything I am truly grateful. So far at least, Fate has dealt me marked cards.

Postscript

Since ending this memoir Fate has suddenly swept up the pack of cards, shuffled, and dealt again. Only this time no one has marked cards. Everyone in the world has picked up a hand whose combined effects will reverberate for decades to come. The history books will doubtless equate the Coronavirus pandemic of 2020 with the Spanish Flu of 1918, if not the diseases and plagues of earlier times. Indeed, this latest pandemic looks likely to colour our attitudes to work and social life, family and friendships, as well as the environment, in ways no other single natural or human-caused act has achieved for centuries.

Never before has the industrialised world's economy been systemically and deliberately frozen to save human life from a previously unknown virus without regard to the cost, with all the future damage to growth and employment which that will entail. Will the temporary respite of isolation prove worse than the disease? After all, it appears that eighty per cent of sufferers only experience mild symptoms. Fatalities in general do not exceed five per cent, in many countries far less. Most deaths occur among the elderly, infirm, often both. Our forefathers would undoubtedly have soldiered on as always until herd immunity, a cure, or a vaccine had been discovered – a mere few months or perhaps a year away. Negative growth and high unemployment is likely to endanger the future mental and physical health of far more than five per cent of a passing generation. Only time will tell which was the right call numerically.

Nevertheless, morally, I prefer to believe that the universal act of compassion to do everything to avoid any further immediate deaths bathes the current state of humanity in a golden light. That the hundreds of thousands of individual, heroic deeds of doctors, nurses, health-care workers, and public servants of all types in every country, serve to show just how far the communal soul of mankind has progressed at last. Gone is the ancient mantra of the survival of the fittest, in favour of the sanctity of all human life. The changes of attitude that will inevitably follow will generally make for a less frantic, cleaner, more caring world. Whilst the temporary abandonment of globalisation for a retreat to the more self-sufficient nation state will rebuild the old bonds of family and community. At least for a while.

It is, however, perfectly clear to me that the stories of my life in this book already belong to a more glamorous, more sophisticated, yet simpler world. A world indeed now gone with the wind. I hope they are, perhaps, the more readable for that.

The End

Acknowledgements

My sincere thanks to Naim Attallah for his continued faith in publishing a second work of mine, and to Mandi Gomez and Hannah Sarid de Mowbray for rationalising its contents. Also, to my wife, Emily, for her encouragement and support, and to our friend Katie Braine who persuaded me to write this book.

Since it is effectively a collection of anecdotes, I hope I have not offended any of our friends by omission. This book essentially ends in the late 1990s, soon after Emily and I were married. In addition, with a couple of exceptions, I have refrained from recounting the odd episode from my earlier years that may embarrass one or two older friends or their families.

MANOLI OLYMPITIS
Kalymnos, Greece, February 2020

Index

Fawcett, Farrah, xi, xii, 57 n.
FIFA World Cup, 1966, 13
Film Finances Inc., 77, 87; *see also*
    Richard Soames
Films:
  Butch Cassidy and the Sundance Kid,
    105
  Dance of the Vampires, 43
  Forrest Gump, 57, 87; *see also* Winston
    Groom
  Freedom at Midnight, 39
  High Noon, 77
  High Society, 65
  Hud, 43
  Indecent Proposal, 133
  Ironweed, 132
  James Bond, 159
  Lenny, 104, 169
  Lipstick, 109
  O Jerusalem!, 39
  Or I'll Dress You in Mourning, 39
  Slaughterhouse Five, 104; *see also*
    Vonnegut, Kurt
  Smiley's People, 33; *see also* Alec
    Guinness
  Sophie's Choice, 132
  Superman I & II, 104 n., 109; *see also*
    Perrine, Valerie
  The Border, 104 n.
  The Bridge on the River Kwai, 77
  The Electric Horseman, 104 n.
  The Fountainhead, 43
  The Guns of Navarone, 77
  The Ipcress File, 25
  The Longest Day, 38
  The Sting, 105
  Tinker Tailor Soldier Spy, 32
  To Kill a Mockingbird, xii
  Town Bloody Hall, 143
  Water, 104
  Witness for the Prosecution, 157;
    157 n.
Finney, Albert, 15

Fishers Island, NY, 65
Flick brothers, 58; Mick, 60
Flynn, Errol, 63–64
Flynn Sean, 64
Ford, Anna, 125; 125 n.
Ford, David, 110
Ford, Henry, 58 n.
Foreign Trade Bank of the Soviet
    Union, 23
Foreman, Carl, 77–78, 92, 96; *see also*
    By Victories Undone
Forman, Miloš, 57 n.
Four Seasons Hotel, Chicago, 70
Frederick's restaurant, Camden
    Passage, London, 28

Gadsden, Sir Peter, 123
Galliers-Pratt, Alibee, 57 n.
Galliers-Pratt, Rupert, 57; 57 n., 76
Galliers-Pratt, Nigel, 76
Gardner, Ava, 15, 42
George club, 35; *see also* Mark Birley
George, Susan, 128
Getty, Paul, 34
Gilbert, Martin, 126
Global Guarantees Inc., 77, 87
Glover, Danny, 133
Gold, Johnny, 18; *see also* Tramp night
    club
Golding, Arnold, 49
Golding, Bernice
Golding, Faith, 68
Golding, Jan, *see* Cushing
Golding, Samuel, 48, 49
Golding Trusts, 49, 68, 88
Goldman Sachs, 154
Gordy, Berry, 113
Gossip columns, *see* Newspapers
Graham, Karen, 93
Graham, Stuart, 117 n., 126
Grant, Cary, 78
Greek Brigade, 4
Greek Jewish community, 4

Spencer-Churchill, Lord Charles, 76
Spencer-Churchill, Lady Jane, 53, 57 n.
Spencer-Churchill, Winston, grandson
　of, also known as Winston
　Churchill, 136–38, 141
Spetsopoula, Greece, 57
Spiegel, Sam, 56 n., 58, 59
Spielberg, Steven, 101
Sponge industry of Kalymnos,
　Greece; Florida, Nassau, Cuba,
　2–4, 31
Spouting Rock Beach Association
　(Bailey's Beach), Newport, RI, 65
Stainton, Sofia, 79, 126
Stallone, Sylvester, 132
Stamp, Terence, 14–15
Sterling National Bank, NY, 49
Sterling (UK currency), 19
Stevens, Lord David, 120, 150–51
Stevens, Lady, 147
Streep, Meryl, 132
Sulzberger family, 62
Surrogate's Court, NY, 69, 71
Swayze, Patrick, 133
Syriani, Aziz, 123 n.

bin Talal, Hussein, King of Jordan, 111
Tarpon Springs, Florida, 3
Tatton, Derbyshire, 9
Taubman, Al, 58 n.
Taylor, Charles, Liberian President,
　157
Taylor, Elizabeth, 18 n., 113, 114
Teamsters' Union, Washington, DC,
　50
Technicolor Inc., 57, 68
Terry, John, 157
Thatcher, Margaret, former UK PM,
　125, 138
Thatcher, Mark, 18
The Brasserie, Fulham Road, 18
Theodoracopoulos, Taki, 149
Theodorou, Argyro, *see* Olympitis

Thyssen, Hans Heinrich (Heini), 46,
　128 n.
Todhunter family:
　Caroline (mother-in-law), 148
　Charles 'Toppo' (brother-in-law), 11,
　156
　Emily (wife), *see* Olympitis
　Michael (father-in-law), 146
Trader Vic's, London Hilton, Mayfair,
　18
Trafford, Diana, 74
Tramp nightclub, London, 6, 18, 42,
　100
Tranwood plc, 118–25
Troubridge, Marie Christine, *see*
　Princess Michael of Kent
TV-am, 125; 125 n.
TV Media shopping channel, Asia
TV series, shows, programmes:
　'Allo, 'Allo!, 159; 159 n
　Andy Pandy, 18
　Are You Being Served?, 159
　Captain Beaky, 159
　Dempsey and Makepeace, 106
　Dynasty, 115
　Johnny Carson Show, 16–17, 58
　Show Me the Money, 155
　Steambath, 104
　The Sooty Show, 18
20th Century Fox, 31, 38
21 Club, NYC, 63
Twiggy (Dame Lesley Lawson DBE,
　née Hornby), 15 n.
Tynan, Kenneth, 55

Universal Studios, LA, 116
University College London, University,
　6, 160

Vaccaro, Brenda, 108
van Zuylen, Baron, Teddy, 30, 38 n.
Vanderbilt family, 65
Veau d'Or restaurant, NYC, 86